Double Devastation Brought
Glorious Transformation

Double Devastation Brought Glorious Transformation

*Memoir of traumatic accounts
while walking through the fires of adversity
victoriously*

Paula Jones

Published by Living Water Book, Christian Division of Butterfly Typeface Publishing House, Little Rock, Arkansas 72201

Livingwaterbooks.org

Print Book Edition 2022

Library of congress cataloging in publication data under

ISBN 9798538057108

The Amplified Bible 1987, The Zondervan Corporation

Please note that Living Water Books of Butterfly Typeface Publishing House capitalizes specific pronouns to scripture referring to the Father, Son, and Holy Spirit, which may differ from some publishers' styles.

Dedication

I dedicate this book primarily to God Almighty, who brought me through the tragedies of my life. Secondly, to my loving husband Larry Jones of 34 years, thank you dear for every time I looked beside me and there you were. I love you with all my heart! Thirdly, to my family those who are resting in the lord and those who are among the living. I want to also acknowledge my pastor Gary Jennings and his wife Danette. They believed in me when I had doubts about myself and allowed me opportunities to teach and share my life in the church.

A special thanks to my wonderful church family at *The Ark of Praise* who always gave words of encouragement as I embarked on the task of putting this book together. Lastly, this book goes out to all the men and women who will be, who have, and are struggling over a crisis that has overwhelmed their lives. I pray you find the strength and courage needed to overcome the victim mentality.

I hope this book will release you from the bondage of fear, shame, guilt, and condemnation that torments your very existence.

Forward

I feel very privileged to write about Paula Jones who is not only my biological sister, but she is also my spiritual sister in the Lord. I am double blessed because of our unique relationship. Paula has been an inspiration in my life. I witnessed the destruction of her life as she ran from The Lord for many years. Upon surrendering her life to Christ, he delivered her from her mess and cleaned her up with the power of the Holy Spirit. I have seen the Lord move on her behalf through some extremely hard times such as the loss of her son Chris who was also my nephew. He was like a little brother to me because we were only six years and five days apart in age.

I was living with Paula when she discovered her son was dead. This crisis opened old wounds and sparked horrible memories of the previous devastation that she'd gone through when she lost her first husband which was Chris' Father.

This horrible devastation is what you will also find in the pages ahead. The murders occurred in their homes, making front-page headlines in the local paper. The loss of her son was much worse and took much longer to process. She had to learn how to cope with the loss.

"In my opinion, to have to bury your own child is the hardest thing a person could ever have to go through. "

My family, Paula, and I give Jesus Christ all the honor, glory, and praise for His unfailing love, mercy, grace, and peace during such a horrible time. Paula would not have made it where she is today without the Lord keeping her through both of these traumatic experiences. I'm thankful that my sister Paula is rooted in the Lord. She was not only tested but overcame the fire with no traces of ever being singed. She has proven that as long as we have our awesome God on our side, anyone can encounter devastation and walk through a glorious transformation.

Preface

C ountless years and days have come and gone for the little girl that used to hide in the neighbor's boat, knowing full well that her mother was calling for her at the top of her lungs. There have been many sunrises and sunsets for the child that used to make and eat mud pies while catching lightning bugs in the dark with the kids next door. She develops into a teenager walking the neighborhood with her best friend. However, the little girl and the silly teenager become a mature woman of God. She has been called into the Kingdom of God as Queen Esther was in The Bible, *for such a time as this*. (Esther 4:14)

The time is now that I share my story and touch briefly on some other precious individuals that have also passed through my life's journey. I have recounted the incidents of my life and the lives of other individuals within the pages of this book for a distinct cause. My life could have never transpired and unfolded the way it did without God placing certain individuals strategically in my path. I thank

God for each one and pray that He blesses beyond their wildest dreams. Some content of this book will be hard to read, and it may even make the tender heart cry. You may find yourself asking God why did these things happen? I know this because that is the emotion I felt.

I wrote this book for two purposes, the first is to bring glory to my Lord and Savior, Jesus Christ, and then the other purpose is to touch humanity with the pains and scars of my life. I hope as you read the pages of this book, and especially if you have been through similar adversities, that you will allow the Holy Spirit to minister to you through my pain. God has taken me on a marvelous journey of healing and transformation as I have allowed Him to extinguish the refining fire of adversity and replace it with the fires of revival that burn brightly through me as a witness to Him.

Contents

Introduction

December should be a glorious celebration with family and friends, not a time for tragedy and devastation. What could have made someone commit such a hennas crime, to take lives so cruelly and unjustly? Who could have let innocence be a witness to such pain and debauchery? How could life become so twisted and torn all in one night? Could life ever be the same after the results of one man's actions, to take lives as if he was the God of the universe? Would life ever be the same for the survivors of a violent crime that affected so many lives?

The lives this brutal crime affected were ripped to shreds, with no remorseful thought. This brutal transgression affected the lives of two innocent children by taking their mother and father away from them when they needed them the most. This sadistic sin affected two mothers by taking away a son and a daughter long before their time. This vicious crime involved a son who would never know how

13

much his father really loved him, who would grow up wondering why life offered him the hand he's been dealt. This inhumane crime would affect a daughter who would grow up not knowing the love of her birth mother and would have unanswered questions that needed answers desperately to go on with her life. Finally, this crime would affect the life of a young girl, that would be a wife and mother one day, then a widow, and a victim of a violent crime the next. A wife who'd have to put the shattered pieces of her life back together and find a new normal!

The woman I speak of is myself, I am sixty-five years old now, but when all this transpired, I was only nineteen, who married and became a mother at sixteen. I was only a child, and I was pregnant having a child because I wanted to please the man that I was so in love with. So, we married young, and we began life at an age when we should have been going to school dances, dates on Saturdays, and getting ready for proms. Instead, I was getting ready to have a baby, to be a mother, and he was getting ready to be a father. We weren't prepared for what would take place in our lives, but we made the best of it.

On this December day, it started like any other day, but the danger was in the air, and neither of us could discern it.

14

The happiness we felt that day would be short-lived as the night sky would descend upon us as we left the safety of family and friends. The expectation I felt as we drove away that day from my mother-in-law's house would soon be cut away by the horrors of what that night would bring. This man's action came as a great surprise to many people, but to some, they thought he might be capable of doing such a thing. The thing I speak of is murder, who knows he may have done it before this because he sure seemed capable of doing some other unspeakable things, such as skinning a goat while it was still alive or holding up a gas station and beating a man nearly to death with a tire tool. There were many times he petrified his family members with his acts of jealous rage and not to mention the abuse he put his wife through before he finally stole her life from her on that fatal night. Why my husband wanted to associate with such a horrible person was not something I could figure out, nor did I want to try to wrap my head around that. I only know that they had been raised together as schoolmates and friends.

I pray as you read my story that if you, the reader, have been through any trauma, crisis, or situation, a victim of any violence, or if you have lost a loved one and the pain you are going through has been unbearable.

I want you to know that I have written this book for you, and I have revealed my scars within the pages so that you may heal by learning through my pain.

To this day, there are a couple of streets in my hometown of Hot Springs, Arkansas, that I have a hard time driving past. The first street is Troupe Street because this is where my first husband and I lived on the night that he and my best friend were shot to death on New Year's Day in the wee hours of the morning in 1977. The other place I have a hard time being in is the vicinity of Central and the corner of West St. Louis Street because this is the place where my only son was found dead in a Federal Express Dropbox in October 1994.

It's not only driving down streets that make me feel uneasy, but it is also the early hours of two to three o'clock in the morning that gives me an eerie feeling as well. I feel weird about those hours because I was awakened by a call informing me that my son was found dead in that Federal Express Drop box. I wish I could turn back the hands of time and make all this craziness disappear or change the outcome. However, this was not and is not possible, so the family members and I must cope with these tragedies to the best of our abilities. Even though it has been forty-five years since the first terrible devastation and twenty-eight years since the second tragic devastation, the families of these victims and I still carry the scars and sometimes it feels as if it happened just yesterday. The house on 103 Troupe Street no longer stands, but occasionally I will drive past the area where it used to be, and I will still get a macabre feeling that will overtake me. It is almost as if the ground of that property is cursed. I have heard it said that when a man is murdered, his blood cries up from the ground for vengeance. I believe that this is true because Genesis 4:10 states: The voice of your brother's blood is crying to me from the ground, (me) in that scripture means God, and the reason the brother's blood is crying out from the ground is because he was murdered. In Numbers 35:33 God commands, "Do not pollute the land where you are." Bloodshed pollutes the land, and atonement cannot be made for the land on which blood has been shed, except by the blood of the one who shed it.

Therefore, if this is true and I believe God's Word to be true, then it means that the land where a murder was committed can never make peace with the Lord except through the death of the one who committed the murder. I got word a couple of years back that the man that pulled the trigger in the wee hours of that New Year's Eve day died in prison. He served two life sentences for murder in the first degree without parole.

I researched what a first-degree murder charge comprises and found out that it means deliberate planning, premeditation, or malice. Deliberate means that the defendant made a clear-headed decision to kill the victim. Premeditation involves showing that the defendant actually thought about the killing before it occurred. Malice requires proof that the defendant did a harmful act without just cause or legal excuse. I also learned that malice could be presumed if the killing was done with a deadly weapon. These definitions are true of that man, so I believe that the ground on which that house stood is cursed.

In fact, I drove past the property just the other day to see if I still got that creepy feeling, and I did. However, I noticed more about the land: it has a huge fence around it, and it is all grown up with weeds, thistles, and thorn bushes. I would say that those are great indications of what the scripture is talking about when it says it is cursed.

Chapter One

Let's Go Party!

Decmber 31, 1976, was New Year's Eve, a night when most people were getting ready to celebrate by saying goodbye to the old year and welcoming the new year in. Parties were taking place all over the town, all over the world for that matter, and excitement was in the air at least, I could feel it. I wanted to go out to a nightclub or hang out at a friend's house to party to welcome the new year. However, little did I know that this night would be one of the most tragic nights of my entire life. I wondered all day long about how I could talk my husband into going and doing something tonight instead of sitting around the house. I thought, please, let's go party; I am so sick of watching television. Although I was only nineteen and way too young to go to a nightclub, I figured I could use my sisters-in-law's ID to get in; after all, I had used it before, and it worked like a charm. My husband and I visited his mother's house, which we did probably every weekend and sometimes two or three times during the week. I didn't mind; I always had a good time after I got out there. I enjoyed talking to my husband's sisters, well, most of the time anyway; they were just good ole' country folks. We usually played card games or watched television. I figured they talked about me when I wasn't there too. Families are great like that. My husband loved his family, and even though they sometimes got into some spats, it turned out all right.

My son Chris, two years old, loved to go out to his grandmothers because he had cousins his age who would come and visit too. I remember when I was trying to potty train Chris, there were times we would be out at his Grandma's, and he learned to use the potty by being told, When you have to pee, go and pee on the chickens in the yard. I can't remember why or who started him doing that, but he and all the other kids would chase the chickens down to pee on them. What a way to be potty trained, but it did help me with getting him to use the toilet, so I guess it wasn't all bad.

When I became pregnant with my son, I think there must have been something in the water because three of my husband's sisters and I were all pregnant simultaneously. I thought that was relatively cool because we could all go to the doctor and experience the joys and pains of pregnancy together. I attended a health department instead of an actual physician and had to be there early in the morning, waiting until the doctors arrived. Most days, it was an all-day affair that made us angry and in a bad mood because there were no comfortable chairs and nothing to do while we sat there endlessly. Having those children all born around the same time was a blessing for my son Chris because he had plenty of playmates when he went to grandma's house. He loved staying so much that he had a crying fit to stay most of the time, usually, I would make him go home. I decided I would let him spend the night on New Year's Eve. I did not realize it until later, but I believe God orchestrated that to save my son's life.

I know now that he would have probably died if he had been with us that night. We finally got ready to leave and head home, so we said our goodbyes and went away. On the way home our conversation was cheerful. We conversed back and forth about what we might want to do that night. I said, "What do you feel like doing because I really don't care." Knowing all the while, I wanted to party, but I did not want to seem too anxious or obvious.

21

My husband suggested, "Well, we could stop by to see Donny and Cathy." Donny smoked weed and enticed my husband to begin while he lived with us. My husband smoked weed, but it was rare, so I said, "Ok, let's go by there." So that's what we did. Although I would have rather gone to a nightclub, my husband was not much for going to those places. I, however, was introduced to the nightclub scene not long before this and liked the idea of going.

Nevertheless, I was a wife and mother foremost, so I did not dare do anything to put that in jeopardy. Even though my husband was beginning to like marijuana and me too for that matter, I still had to keep my image up, one that was good and clean. I would smoke, but I liked having cocktails or dancing at the clubs. I had a taste for that kind of lifestyle, and I wanted to experiment with it more. I was only a teenager when I went to my first club, so I used my sister-in-law's military ID, and believe me she looked nothing like me. My husband and I walked through the club door with several friends, and of course, they carded me. I showed the ID and was let in with no questions asked.

I was so excited that I could get in and we had such a good time that night. We danced and enjoyed the band so much, and I desired that again. We finally got to Donny and Cathy's house, pulled in the driveway, got out and knocked on the door. Harrison said, "Hey, dude what's going on?" Donny said, "Not much, just drinking a few beers come on in and drink a beer with us." Harrison said, "Thanks and I got something to ask you too. I came by to see if you had anything you'd want to get rid of?"

Donny said, "I got something you might like." Harrison said, "Ok, thanks, man." We stayed for a little while, just long enough to drink a beer and then we went home. Donny and Cathy kept trying to talk my husband into coming back later and coming to the New Year's Eve party they were having at their house. Oh God, how I wished we would have come back, but he just kept saying no, so we finally left and went home.

After we got home, my husband rolled up the joint and smoked some. He said, "Take a hit of this." I said, "I'd rather have a beer or something." He said, "I know what we can do."

I asked, "What?"

Harrison said, "We can go by to see if Jerry Don and Pam are at home. They might want to party with us. We can go by the liquor store and grab some beer get whatever you and Pam might want to drink." I said, "That sounds like a great idea!"

Finally, I thought I was going to have some fun. I really enjoyed talking to Pam; she was fun to get drunk with. I remember several times before Jerry and Pam left to go to North Carolina, they would come over and we would party. We arrived at their home and Jerry Don came to the door. He said, "Hey, what are you guys doing? Come on in." I wish we had never gone through that door and embraced that night. I wished we would have stayed home, smoked those joints, got high, made love, and passed out. Life could be a lot different right now if we had made that choice, but we did not. We walked in the door, and the first thing I noticed was that the house was in an enormous mess and you could feel the tension in the air. Jerry Don was in the living room and Pam was already in bed.

As I think about it now, that seemed somewhat strange to me, because it was probably only between seven and eight o'clock in the evening. Baby Jennifer was asleep in the baby bed in the room with Pam, and Pam seemed irritated and put out with Jerry Don.

Harrison said, "We thought you guys might want to go to the liquor store, get some beer or whatever, and come over to the house and see the New Year in. You guys can spend the night." Jerry Don said, "Oh, we couldn't do that." My husband and I both asked, "Why not?"

Jerry Don said, "Well, if it's not a bother, sounds fun."
Harrison said, "Alright, get up, get dressed, and get your
party on. "What will we do with the baby?" Pam asked.
I said, "Oh, she can be with us; we won't get so wasted where
we can't take care of her."

"Alright, let me get her some clean clothes and diapers,"
Pam said. I helped her get things together. We got the baby
ready, put some clothes in a bag, and were off for our night
of fun, or so we thought. I always loved Pam and hated
seeing her so unhappy; she was my best friend, and I knew
when something was bothering her. My first remembrance
of Pam was going to church with her; she would invite me
to go where her dad preached now and again. I remember
going and Pam would lead the song service, this girl had a
set of lungs that would shake the rafters. I always envied that
in her, because although my voice was ok, it was no
comparison to hers. We were in the choir together at school
and were also a part of The Madrigals, a choir group above
the regular choir that went and sang at different events. That
was part of our school activities.

I remember singing at events at the big auditorium in town
that was so fun because we got to walk around the city on
our breaks.

How I Met My Husband

It was because of her I met my husband; she fixed me up on a blind date with him. I remember when she asked me if I wanted to go out with one of Jerry Don's friends. She told me he was nineteen with a job and a souped-up muscle car. He owned a 1969 SS Chevelle, and you could hear it coming about a mile down the road. I said why not; I will go out with him. I was only fifteen when I went on my first date with him. Harrison came to my house one Friday night and was such a gentleman that he got out of his beautiful car, came to my mom, introduced himself to her, and asked if he could take her daughter out. My mother was very impressed with him and said ok almost immediately. I remember wondering what he looked like and thinking he must be a dog if he must get fixed up on a blind date; then I thought I'm a blind date too so I must be a dog as well. I found out he wasn't a dog in fact, he was very handsome with beautiful blue eyes and thick curly brown hair.

I ended up being very infatuated with him, I might have gone out the first time with him because I thought he was cute with a hot car, but the car was just a plus. I remember I would start listening for him when it was about time for him to be there, and sure enough, here he would come, pulling into the driveway. I also thought I was something when he would pick me up from school in the afternoons. I would think eat your hearts out popular chicks. You have nothing on me. I was ecstatic and more excited about the car than anything else.

My husband, Harrison, was the brother of nine siblings. He came from a large family, and his parents were hard-working country people. My husband loved family and cars. When I met him, he worked at a sawmill, but his heart was for auto mechanics. He was very good at it. I saw him do some miraculous things with vehicles. He could identify problems, and repair and replace parts easily. He had excellent diagnostic skills and could problem-solve quickly.

He loved to roll up his sleeves and get under a vehicle's hood to find out what makes it do what it can do. He didn't mind getting his hands dirty and experimenting with different things to get a car operating at its maximum potential. He loved going to the stock car races, and there was one particular time he surprised me by entering in a race. We had a souped-up Camaro that he'd been working on but the next thing I knew our Camaro was sitting in the lineup to race. He never said a word about entering that contest, and I filmed it but was also afraid. He ended up coming in fourth place, which I thought was pretty good, considering he had no prior experience. I was still upset, but I was proud of him too. I think I realized where my son got some of his rebellious ways. Anyway, back to the main story.

The Unforgettable Night

We pulled in at the liquor store that New Year's Eve night and got what we would drink that night. They got stuff to make Sloe Gin Fizzes for us girls and got beer for them to drink. We pulled away from the liquor store and were going down the road in our pickup truck. We no longer had the hot car by this time. We were piled up in that truck, us four and baby Jennifer. I remember being really cramped up in there, but that was an external matter to prelude what was really bothering me. The fact of being cramped up did not bother me as badly as the conversation coming out of Jerry Don's mouth about how many fatalities they predicted for that night. I thought little about it then, but the warning signs were there. There were several warning signs if we just had the smarts back then to put the puzzle pieces together. I remember a few weeks back as my husband and Jerry don picked me up from work. Jerry started talking about how he thought going to prison wouldn't be half bad. You would get a place to stay, three square meals, and the men in there didn't have to work that hard. Those were his exact words. However, I was young and did not think about things as I think now. I have said many times that if I could go back

28

with what I know now, I would do so much differently. I promise you, as God Almighty is my witness, and I say that with the deepest of reverence and gratitude, I would surely do things differently.

We pulled into the driveway of our house and got out of the truck. Pam got baby Jennifer pacified, and I started getting our drinks going. Pam entered the kitchen where I was, and we started talking about many things. Pam and Jerry had just returned from North Carolina; they hadn't been in town for long, maybe a couple of weeks. She told me she had been working as a cocktail server and how the money was fantastic if you were friendly and talked with the men how they like to be talked to. I thought if your daddy knew, he would have a cow. After all, he was a Baptist minister. We finally went into the living room, where the guys sat, drinking their beers and talking. We joined in on the conversation they were having.

My husband finally asked, "Would anyone want to get high?" Jerry and Pam were astonished because this was something new for my husband; they had never known him to smoke weed. Jerry said, "I don't think I do. I have never done that stuff."

"Oh, it won't hurt you just try a couple of hits; you'll see, you'll like it!" my husband exclaimed. Pam said, "Same here." My husband kept on at us until we all did a hit or two. It was some good stuff because it hit us fast. I recall we did not make it to see the New Year in; because we were all just wiped out, it happened pretty fast. We got ready for bed and made Jerry Don and Pam a pallet in the living room. The house we lived in was like a shotgun house. It was one long straight shot. The house had a living room, dining room that we used for our bedroom, kitchen, and bath that was one straight shot. Then it had a downstairs with three more bedrooms that we did not use except for storage.

I wanted to move out of this house several times because I felt that there was some demonic activity, or the house was haunted or something. The house was just creepy; I would wake up in the middle of the night and see like a black form standing over my bed. I had always been raised to know God and reverence Him. I knew I could call on Jesus if I were scared, and He would help me. So, when I saw shadows, even though I was not a professed Christian, I would call on the name of Jesus, turn my head to the wall and go to sleep.

I had odd feelings that would come over me even during the middle of the day. I would be doing household chores and the oddest feeling would overwhelm me, and I would have to get my baby and go sit out in the lawn chair until my husband got home from work. Everyone who came to visit would have a weird feeling to come over them, especially when they stood at the top of the stairs. I don't know a lot about demonic activity residing in a house, but if I was a betting person, I would put all my money on the fact that there was something in that house. I wrote this part of the book to help others understand what's about to happen and how it didn't make any sense.

The part I am about to share in this book is the absolute hardest for me because it is so painful to remember. I share this story because I know that is what God wants me to do and for no other reason. I do not want to bring hurt, disgrace, or shame on anyone, whether they are alive or deceased. Believe me, that is not my intention. However, if this story will help someone who is struggling to understand why they had to go through the pain of loss and what I went through can help them cope or to know that they are not alone, then it is what I need to do. I would love to write about how we went to sleep, woke up the next day and went on with life as usual but that was not the case.

My husband and Jerry Don wanted to do something that disgusted me, that I wanted to leave it out of this story, but I can't. I have left it out too many times, I must tell it all for it to be effective. Wife-swapping is not something that I am proud of, and I wish it wouldn't have happened, but it did. I have buried this for so long that I do not know if I can bring it to the surface without causing so much pain within me. However, I must tell it because God will use this to set others free.

This act happened a couple of times before this night; I hated when my husband approached me with it. He would beg me to participate in this, but I could never bring myself to do such a horrible thing. Harrison had no problem with it and it's possible that it cost him his life. I just don't know. I could never do it and I would pull away from Jerry Don's advances toward me. I would see my husband and Pam, from the other side of the room together having sexual intercourse and it was so hurtful. Jerry Don would keep trying to get me to do it with him, but I would not. I would tell him no and this night was no different. I tried to get my husband not to do this, but he was determined. I, however, was determined that I would not do that. I was never raised like this, and I knew that was very wrong.

Chapter Two

The Sound of Gunfire

I can't remember going to sleep; I only know that we did. The next thing I recall as I lay beside my husband sleeping was being awakened to a sound and a burning on my left shoulder. I heard another sound, and I knew it was gunfire. I was still trying to figure out what was going on. I could feel myself trying to get up, and I heard Pam scream, "Jerry!" Two more gunshots were fired then there was silence. By this time, I was up on the side of the bed, wondering what was going on! I raised my head, and I immediately saw the barrel of a shotgun pointed right at my head! Jerry Don was standing over me with a gun pointed at me, and I knew I would die! He said, "Don't you move, or I will blow your brains out! They are not dead, so don't worry about it! Just do what I tell you to do, and I won't kill you!" I was petrified, but I still was not sure about what happened. I could feel my arm burning and it occurred to me later that it was powder burns from where my husband had been shot the first time as I laid beside him sleeping. Jerry Don made me do some horrible things to my husband that I am to ashamed to even speak of. He told me to turn my husband over and he said, "Now I want you to go down on him! Do it!" He screamed. I did not have a choice. I hated him so bad by this time, but what could I do other than do what he told me to do? He was twice as big as me and had a shotgun in his hands, my husband's shotgun. Then he screamed at me, "Do you not know what I am talking about? Come on, put it in your mouth!" I turned my husband's body over and did what I was told. Then he shouted at me, "Stop!" He said, "Get dressed, well, wait. I want to pick out what you are going to wear." So, he picked out a pair of pants and a button-up shirt for me to wear. "Put these on!" He commanded. I did what he told me to do and didn't ask questions. He told me to put them on slowly. He watched me dress; he made me feel so nasty. He touched me on my breast and other areas. I couldn't figure out what he was thinking or why he did this horrible thing. Then he just stopped and told me to finish getting dressed.

I was thankful that he stopped what he was doing. After I got dressed, he asked, "Where is Harrison's wallet?"

"I don't know," I said.

I couldn't imagine what he was thinking or why he wanted my husband's wallet only to take what money we had, and that wasn't much. It seemed we always struggled financially. We both worked and made money, but it just didn't seem to go anywhere. Our priorities were probably a little whacked as well.

"You better find it!" Jerry Don said as he screamed into my ear! I couldn't remember where my husband put it before going to bed, and I thought it might be in the kitchen. He was yelling at me and pointing the gun at my chest while telling me they weren't dead when I knew by this time that they were. I just couldn't think then I screamed, "It might be in the kitchen!"

He said, "It better be, go look and don't try anything funny." Well, how can you try anything funny in a shotgun house he could see my every move. I went into the kitchen and saw the wallet lying on the table, and I grabbed it up and exclaimed, "I found it!"

He told me his plans about how he would take me to North Carolina and make a prostitute out of me, then, when he had made enough money off of me, he would kill me. First, he said that he had some more people that he wanted to kill, one being my son and my husband's family. He also said he would kill a couple of friends of his and my husband's and he needed all of Harrison's ammunition. My husband loved to hunt, and he had about three guns: rifles or shotguns. I'm not sure; I knew nothing about guns.

He gathered up all the guns then made me carry two of them. As I walked through the living room, I remember stepping over Pam's body. I tried to look, and he screamed, "Don't look at her." I saw baby Jennifer on the couch I wondered what was going through her little mind. Then I heard him say, "Leave her there, she will be fine."

I didn't know if I would make it to the truck carrying those guns; they seemed so heavy. Suddenly he saw my son's penny bank sitting on a shelf in the living room. He screamed, "Get that penny bank!" I thought, what can you do with a penny bank because there wasn't much money in there? However, I didn't argue, I just did as I was told. It was the hardest thing to put one more thing in my arms. I had guns, a sack of ammunition, and a penny bank. To top it off, when I got to the truck, he told me to open the truck door. I don't know how I did all these things, except God had to be with me. I finally got the truck door open and somehow got in the truck. He got in the truck and started it up. He made me sit in the middle beside him, and I felt horrible. He kept making me say that I was his girl.

"Tell me you're my girl." I thought, no, I can't do this! I knew I had to do what he told me to do if I wanted to live.

So, I could hear the words come out of my mouth, but they were ever so weak.

"I'm your girl!" I sobbed. Then I heard him say you better say it right and like you mean it, or it won't be good for you. I said again, "I'm your girl!!" So, he drove a little further down the road towards town and then he said, "Pull your pants down!" I looked at him and I didn't understand.

"Pull your pants down!" He screamed at me and said, "You better do what I tell you to do! "I pulled them down, and he turned my face toward me and kissed me. I thought, oh my God I can't stand this. Then suddenly, he slapped me in the face so hard. I'd never been hit or slapped by a man. "Pull your pants back up and don't you ever do anything like that again! You're my girl and no one else's and you had better get used to it!" I knew I had to get away from him if I wanted to live, and I was so afraid of what would happen next.

I just did not have a clue what he was capable of doing next. He put the truck in gear and pulled out of the drive. He kept talking about who he would kill and where we were going. Some things he said made little sense to me at all. I just knew I would die that night if I didn't get away from him. We finally stopped at a gas station on the other side of town, and I was so thankful we stopped, but I didn't know how I would get away from him. Suddenly he told me I would have to go in and pay for the gas. I thought this had to be my chance if I am to live; I have to get away from him here. I was so afraid, but I knew I had to do something if I didn't, I would die soon. He stepped out of the truck to pump the gas and as he did, he said.

"Go in and pay for the gas and do nothing stupid!" He exclaimed. I lied and said, "I won't!" My adrenaline was flying. I went to the gas station and there was an older couple there. They took my money and while they were taking it, I told them I needed help.

"Call the police, please! This man is going to kill me! He has already killed two other people. Please call the police. Help me, please, I beg you!"

The woman said, "Don't worry, we will help you."

"Please hurry!" I was so afraid I knew he would come in here in a minute because I was taking too long. The man began dialing the phone, and I could see Jerry Don coming from the gas pump. "Oh God, he is coming!" They told me to get over there, and they would deal with it. The police will be here in just one minute. He came into the store, and he could still get to me from where I was. He started grabbing for me, and I fought with all my might.

"You come here you little bitch, I am going to kill you for this!" I struggled even harder it seemed I had the strength of

38

ten men. He grabbed me again, and this time he grabbed my shirt right off me. He kept screaming at me and calling me names. Suddenly out of the corner of my eye I saw these gallon glass jugs of milk in a cooler and fighting him all the way I finally got to the cooler. I opened the door, grabbed one, and threw it at him with all my might. He slammed me up against the cooler; and my head hit the corner of it hard. Blood began flowing down my head, and I couldn't feel anything because I was fighting for my life. Someone told me later I should have had stitches; to this day, I still have an indention in my head.

About that time, I heard sirens coming, and he did too. He said, "I will come back for you and finish you if it takes me the rest of my life! You are dead! You got that bitch!" I believed him, too after all, he had just killed two people why wouldn't he kill me? He ran out of the store, and I saw him jump in my husband's truck to take off. About the time he took off, four squad cars came barreling in the parking lot. I could see the man and woman directing the cops and telling them what had just transpired, and then I see two cop cars take off after him while two stayed questioning me.

I was standing in the middle of the parking lot of a gas station with my chest exposed to the entire world, and finally someone gave me my shirt back. I felt so violated. Rape couldn't be any worse than this. I told them the address, and they put me in one of the squad cars, and they told me to direct them to the place of residence. I told them that there was a baby still in that house and they began driving to the scene of the crime even faster. We pulled up to the house, and I got out. I was going to go in, but they stopped me.

The police officer said, "You can't go in there. Stay back! Where is your husband?" the police officer asked.

"He is in bed," I answered. I wondered why they would ask me that; couldn't they see? I found out later that someone said they found my husband's body in the kitchen, but I am not sure. I dare say if that was the case, then he wasn't dead when I was there with that maniac. If Jerry Don had known that he would have reshot him. They handed Jennifer out to me through the door and told me to go sit in the squad car. So, I did what they said, I was still afraid, and baby Jennifer was crying. The police officers finally got in the car and drove to the police station. In the meantime, a high-speed chase took place in pursuit of Jerry Don, and they finally caught up to him and apprehended him.

When I gave my testimony at the police station, I could hear them bringing him in. I thought, I don't want to see him. Oh please, God, don't let me see him! Thank God, they brought him through without me having to make eye contact with that maniac! I gave my statement and said, "I need someone to call my mother and my husband's mother."

I can't remember how it happened; all I know is my stepfather appeared at the station to get me.

Glorious Transformation Tips

COURAGE TO OVERCOME

It takes courage to share something so scary with someone you love so much! Yet it is still important to look fear in the eyes and say, I'm courageous in the truth I live in!

Chapter Three

Rescued from Pain, Remembering the Shame

When I saw my stepfather, I remember grabbing his coat and telling him that Harrison was dead and that Jerry Don killed him. It was a big deal for me to grab his coat because I disliked the man with everything in me. The reason is that he touched me where a father should never touch his teenage daughter. I remember this happening several times when I was a young teenager until I finally got the courage to tell my mother what he was doing. However, next to what I had just been through, I disliked him less than the other maniac I had just been rescued from. The next thing I remember is that I was at my mother's house.

The days and weeks ahead were very strenuous. I made it through this nightmare by the grace of God and my mother's prayers. My mother's house was not a place I wanted to be in fact I got married young to get away from it because of the shame of molestation and being under the rule of my stepfather who seemed to be a horribly mean man. However, I loved my siblings and they are the reason that I tolerated everything for as long as I did. I tried to stay away from there because of all the confusion and commotion that occurred. However everything brought back memories including living at my parents house again adjusting to life.

Reflecting On Life With Him

As my mind reflects, I can recall how my husband and I had a talk about moving away from my parent's house one night when he and I were in our usual parking place. We were talking about marriage, having his baby, and how it would be to finally be together forever. I thought how wonderful because I loved him so much and I never wanted to be with anyone else anyway. Neither of us knew what genuine love was, but I knew I loved him as much as I could identify with genuine love. We made love that night and I believe with all my heart this was the night I became pregnant with our son. This was the fall of the year when I became pregnant and before Christmas, we were married.

44

We had a little wedding at my sister's house, nothing fancy, but it was magical, and I was the happiest girl in the entire world. We got in the car after the wedding and circled the fountain uptown with his family and friends behind us honking. After we finished driving through town we went with his sister and her husband to the A & W to eat and get a root beer. We finally made it to the hotel room and got out of the car that was all decorated by the guys. We got our suitcases out of the car and went in the room. The room was awesome, and as my husband sat on the bed there was the sound of cowbells. I was like what is that. He looked under, and someone got into our room and tied a cowbell to the bed. I wish I could tell you that was all they did but no they put salt between the sheets of the bed, Vaseline on the toilet seat and took all the towels out of the bathroom. This made things very uncomfortable, but we still figured out a way to enjoy our wedding night and I was so happy.

My happiness ended the next morning when we woke, and he told me he had a confession to make. I was so happy I thought there's nothing he could confess to that could hurt me so bad where I could not get through. He told me that he slept with another girl the night before we were married. He confessed the girl was pregnant and that what they did caused her to lose the child she was carrying.

I was so upset that I thought I would die and wanted to leave and return home. He said, "I didn't want to tell you before we got married because I was afraid you wouldn't marry me; Forgive me!" Well I did forgive him, partly because of our son and partly because I loved him so much. I knew if I listened long enough, I would believe him even though he lied in my face while I cried. I still searched for reasons to believe. I know this sounds like a Rod Stewart song; However, I knew this would not be the last time he cheated, and there would be other times for me to learn to forgive and look for reasons to believe.

I believed in my husband, and so many good qualities in him made me love him so much. With all his faults, my husband was a very kind man who loved his family, and I knew he loved me. When I met his family, his father was very sick and in the hospital. I remember us going to the hospital to see him and his Mother would be there caring for my husband's father. I saw this man for the first time in a hospital bed, fighting for his life. I recall him lying there and doing motions with his hands like he was winding a rod and reel. I asked, "What is your Father doing?" and He said, "He's fishing."

My husband's father passed away not long after that, and I remember going to the funeral and then out to the family's house to pay respect. The things I saw there were very foreign to me because I had never seen a family act the way this family did after a funeral. The men were drinking beer and there were a lot of loud discussions, arguing, and fussing going on. I really didn't understand that entire scenario, and I was glad we didn't stay long. I think my husband may have been a little embarrassed by what I was having to witness. I know my husband loved his family, and it broke his heart that he lost his Dad. He was in pain because he did not have his dad in his life at anymore. I understood his pain because I also had issues within my family that were not at all that pleasing.

Living With My Parents Again

The issues that I had to deal with are what made me realize that after this tragic chaotic incident that I could not live life the same as before. I also knew in my heart I did not want to go back to my mother's house because of my step-father and the hells of that household. I do remember many happy times when things were actually good. My mother and step-father seemed very good together. I just know that her life differed greatly from the life that she had with my father. I had no intention of going back there, no matter how difficult it was for me to endure the news.

People say my real father was a wonderful man, a hard worker, and that he loved his family. I wish I could have known him, but he died because of health reasons when I was about four years old. Thus I have no remembrance of this wonderful man. He loved my mother and made a wonderful home for her, and always provided for us kids. They say that the day he died he had candy in his pocket to give me when he got home. That makes me cry when I think of it. After his death, my mother remarried and for a while it was good. I remember this man holding me and treating me like an actual father should treat his child. I was always treated very well. My mother dressed me in the finest clothes that she could afford, and I never went without anything, really. The only real things that I ever got in trouble for really is not coming when she called for me, leaving my tricycle behind the car, and playing school on the side of the house with crayons.

However, when my mother became pregnant with my stepfather's children, I quickly became the stepchild. Things change drastically in the house for me. I was not special anymore, and I do not even think he wanted me there. I was made fun of for being hungry and eating too much and he ridiculed me for so many things that I just got to where I didn't speak to anyone too much. I learned to play games by myself or I would make mud pies with the neighbor girl next door. Until one day, the neighbor girl wanted to play doctor underneath our house and it made me feel creepy because she pulled my pants down and put rocks in my private place. I got away from her as fast as I could and never played with her again! I never told my mother about the neighbor girl however, I got the courage to tell her about what my stepfather had been doing to me; I know she wanted to leave this man, but in those days, a woman with five small children did not have anywhere to go, really. She worked as a housekeeper and had no money really and could get no help, so she had to stay with this man and it was horrible in the household. There was always a big fuss and fight going on among someone or about something.

After my husband's murder, I remember people coming over to my mother's house to comfort me and to pay their respects. They all had their questions, and I did not feel like talking. In fact, after a while I quit receiving guests at my mother's house, it was just too painful. I spent a lot of time in my bedroom just sitting and looking at the walls, wondering what I was going to do with my life. On the day of the funeral it was early January, and it was kind of cold yet it didn't seem to be that bad or maybe I just couldn't feel the cold for the pain within my heart. I recall the trip to the cemetery and there seemed to be many people around me yet I still felt isolated and alone. I made it through the major service but couldn't attend the gravesite. My legs buckled under me as I tried to walk to where everyone else was, and I felt everyone's eyes on me. It was more than I could stand. I felt like I was losing it and that my life was hopeless. I sat there wondering how I could go on. This can't be real. I felt myself losing control, and then it happened I fell out. Suddenly one of my husband's brothers grabbed me up, and I was sitting in a car before I knew it. I was thankful someone was looking out for me.

Chapter Four

Trying to Find A New Normal

I finally convinced myself that it was time I went back to work. I dreaded the first day back there, but I had to get back into reality after all; I had a son to raise and knew I had to find a new normal for my life if I was going to make it emotionally and financially. I worked at a shoe factory that employed around two hundred people, and I knew that as soon as I walked through that big double door, all eyes were going to be on me. I could just imagine all the talk and all the questions that everyone had. I worked there long enough to know that this was a place with all kinds of gossip about people all the time. I knew beyond a shadow of a doubt that people would talk about this for a long time.

After all, it was front-page news, and I am sure everyone had their suspicions and stories about why my husband and his wife were killed. I mustered up the courage to shove those doors open and walk back to my department. I worked in the sewing department of the shoe factory, which was at the back of the building. My job was called Assemble Mocc, where the top two parts of the shoes were glued and assembled together at the toe. I liked my job and I was actually the first that had ever made their quota while doing this job. To explain quota, it is the amount done that would add up to making minimum wage for that day and the amount over would increase per hour. The shoe factory I worked at paid its employees by the pieces of work so it was very important to meet the quota for the day. The supervisor made a video of me putting a shoe together so that others could learn how to do this job. I believe that they used that video for several years after I quit working there. I felt proud and accomplished that they made a video of me doing that. No one said anything to me right off when I went back to work, which was nice because I did not want to talk to anyone. I just wanted to go to work and go home; I didn't need any new friends because I could not trust people.

A Chance to Express

Finally, people started expressing how sorry they were about what had happened to me. I told them thank you but never had any real discussions with anyone, not even my good friends Karen and Diana. Until one day, my friend

Diana met me in the work parking lot while walking to my car. She had a bottle of wine and two glasses and she said, "Let's go talk." I said, "What do you mean?" I knew what she meant but did not want to talk about it; I just wanted to forget it. She said, "You have been quiet for way too long about what happened to you and I want you to talk to me." I struggled with what she was saying. I made excuses like I needed to get home and tended to Chris. However, she was not having any of it; she was a great friend and knew I was hurting so inside. I knew it too; my guts felt like they were churning in me most of the time, and the emotional pain was sometimes unbearable. I did not know then but after I studied psychology and all the different psychological abnormal behaviors; I discovered I suffered from Post-Traumatic Stress Disorder. I was too young and naïve to know that I needed to be seen by a therapist or counselor. I wish I had someone that could have directed me in this because the other road to recovery I chose was not the road I should have ever gone down.

Finally, I turned to Diana and said, "Ok, where are we going?" She said, "We can go to the lake park if you want to." I thought, well, I don't think she's giving me a choice, really. So, I said, "Ok." I got in her car, and we arrived at the park. The park was a place where you could drive down to the dock and fish or swim. It had a nice parking lot and a playground with tables large enough to have a picnic.

There we sat in the car as Diana opened the bottle of wine and poured us both a glass as we talked. I talked, and I cried. I talked and I cried some more until we needed more wine. I couldn't help but think… God, I needed this release. She was right I needed this therapy desperately. It felt so good to get some of that out of me finally. Oh God, it had been bottled up until I thought I would explode!

Diana and I became closer after I shared all of that with her. My husband never wanted me to have any friends, especially Diana. She would invite us over to her house on the weekends, but he never wanted to go. However, she became my drinking buddy after he died, and we always went out together. If you saw her, you saw me and man we always had a good time together. She was seeing a guy whose parents owned a bar in town called, "The Horseshoe Bar." We would go there before going to the nightclubs because drinks were free, and we could get our buzz started. The guy she was seeing had a brother; they always cared for us when we were there. They never let any man take advantage of us.

Diana and this guy dated and lived together for many years. They cared for each other a lot, and you could tell from how they interacted. However, their relationship was cut short because he was killed one night in a bar tragically. I lost contact with her after this happened. I was thankful for her helping me come out of my shell, and I understood what she was trying to do even though her ethics were still not what I needed in my life. I saw Diana as an awesome friend and I knew she really cared for me. I tried reaching out to her after I started going to church so we could go to church together again, but it seemed like our friendship just fell apart. I heard she ran off the bridge on the same road she lived on and was killed. It was quite a shock, and it hurt my heart for her.

Rest in Peace my friend, Diana.
I prayed that she made peace with God,
and I hope to see you again in Heaven

Shortly after the transition of my friend Diana, I heard Harrison's mother passed away. The news about her death took its toll on me, and my relationship with my husband's family weighed heavy on me as well. They helped me to get through some tough times in my life but I could always feel the separation. My Mother-in-law would talk to me and say that I was welcome there anytime, but I still found it hard to reach out to her as I should have. I loved her and held her in high regard, but I knew that part of my life had ended. I had one goal: to get my life back to normal.

One of my husband's sisters helped me to get some aid because I was a widow with a child. I applied for Social Security benefits and it was about six months before they approved me for survivor's benefits. I received back pay for the six months I had to wait for my checks to get started, which helped me have a pretty good down payment on a new car. I remember being excited because it was the first nice thing to happen to me since the tragedy. I bought my first brand new car, a 1977 Oldsmobile Cutlass Supreme white on white; two-door Coupe. Oh my God, it was nice! I felt like I was on top of the world, but it didn't last long.

I wanted to show off my car, so I drove it out to my husband's mother's house, and I remember bouncing in the door and telling them, "I got a new car!" I thought they were going to be so excited and go for a ride. However, they were not, nor would they look at it. I felt like a fool. I now understand their feelings, but I was terribly upset then. I know now that they felt that what got me that new car was blood money. The price paid for my car was the life of their son and brother. I left that day and didn't go out there again for a long while. I didn't understand then because I was very young. I was only nineteen.

Chapter Five

My New Life

This new life I carved out and began living was filled with a lot of fun and adventurous times. I thought this was going to be great. I thought to myself, I will get an apartment and soon my son and I will be fine. I missed my husband, and I wished that night would have never happened; it did and somehow, I was going to have to make the best of what my life was now.

The preliminary hearing was very painful, and I knew that I would have to see this man in the courtroom. I wasn't looking forward to it at all. However, there was no big trial, although my husband's family and I wanted to go to trial. We ended up reading in the newspaper that they had plea-bargained and given him life in prison with no parole. I didn't like it; I questioned the prosecuting attorney about it, but they had their excuses. I tried to keep a relationship with my husband's family; I stayed close to a couple of his sisters and their families. I would visit with them. We'd party together and have a great time. One of my husband's sisters lived with me for a while, which was nice but didn't last. I understood their view that being around Chris and me was too painful. We were a reminder of their brother and the memories that circled us were a reflection of him. I lived with my sister for a while, which was good but I had to hear lecturers every time I made plans to go out with my friends or another man. This was almost worse than living with my mother. However, sometimes my mother would come over to my sisters and I'd hear it from both of them. My sister said, "Watch whom you're associating with and wait before getting serious about any other man." They warranted all these fears, and I truly needed to listen. I listened more to myself and other people who were not my friends more like fair-weather friends.

Old Enough To Decide

I loved my mother and sister very much, but I was a grown woman with needs and desires. I was old enough to choose what I wanted but was also so stupid and my choices were so negative. They each had such a terrible impact on my life. For example, I decided to start going back to the clubs and drinking every chance I got because this was how I dealt with the pain and horrors of what happened to me.

I admit I was very gullible and got into one bad relationship after the other. I mainly did this because of all my fears of never wanting to be alone. I left my sister's house and rented my own house so I could do what I desired. I met several men that I went out with and one that I got involved with pretty heavily. I was so head over heels that I quit my job and went to California with him and his friend on just a whim. This was one of the craziest things ever. I believe that I was so hurt and devastated by past events that I tolerated lies, searching for happiness. This kind of thinking made me vulnerable to many things and people.

I remember getting a few clothes together and my son then off we went. The man took one of his buddies with him and we headed out. I never found out what they were running from but I believe they were definitely running from something. I often think that maybe they broke the law somehow and used me to get out of town for a while in my brand-new car. Heaven only knows because he never really shared anything with me about it. This man was so inconsiderate of me; he did not respect my child or me. He stayed drunk the entire time and, of course, asked to do most of the driving. He passed other cars like they were sitting still; sometimes, he would pass other cars from the shoulder side of the road.

He was driving at higher speeds that it was a wonder we did not wreck, killing ourselves or others. Again, God was with me through this and kept me in the grip of His grace.

The Truth On The Trip

I saw a lot of California. I saw the San Francisco Bridge, the Hollywood sign in Los Angeles, San Diego Park, The Capitol Studio Building, Hollywood, and Vine Street. I remember driving on Ventura 101 Freeway, and it was a nightmare because it's five lanes going one way. You must get at a speed of about eighty miles per hour and stay there at that speed. We went on Highway 101, which followed the beach line of the Pacific Ocean; it was beautiful. We stopped at the ocean and walked around on the beach. The scenery was so beautiful. I hoped to return and take it all in again. We ended up following this road to Monterey, California, and this is where we stopped because he had some family up there, so we lived with them. This town was exquisite, it had cobblestone streets in some areas, and the beach was beautiful. The trip ended when his family discovered he was not divorced yet, living in their home with a woman and child (us). I did not know at the time that he was married and an alcoholic. He told me he was separated and getting a divorce. The truth was that his wife was just out of town visiting relatives. At this moment, I found out he had no intentions of divorcing his wife. He used me, and I was so embarrassed. The people were not mad at me in fact they gave me money so I could get back to Hot Springs, again this was yet another turn showing that God was with me.

The outcome of this crazy venture in my life is that I ended up driving back from California with my son and me all by myself. The other man traveled with us for a while but ended up getting off in one of the towns where we stopped for gas. He was trying to make advances toward me as we traveled but I told him I was not interested. He left after that and I was thankful he never tried to hurt me or be mean to me while we were traveling. I was so happy to see the out skirts of Hot Springs when we came in off the Little Rock highway. God's mercy kept me. I was so very undeserving of it. As I think back, I was so blind to the reality of what this man was. He was an alcoholic and a womanizer. I found out that he was no longer married and was killed tragically while driving log trucks.

Glorious Transformation Tips

God Can Turn A Mess Into A Message

I could not figure out why God saved me and let me live. I was a mess, but I know now God can make a message out of our messes. He is stronger than anything we go through, or any demon that is holding us captive.

Chapter Six

Delving Deeper into Sin

After this man did a number on my head, I began to really get a crusted outer shell around me that was hard for anyone to penetrate. I delved deeper into the party life and met another man during this time. I immediately moved in with him because I needed someone to take care of me. There was very little love in this for me. I cared for him but did not love him because if I had I would have never done the things I did to him. All I wanted is for someone to take care of me because I was doing a horrible job of it myself, although I thought I knew everything.

My older brother called me and told me how wrong I was for living in fornication with this man and how horrible my life would be if I kept this lifestyle up. However, I told my brother I was in love, but I did not even know what real love was. I did not need a relationship right now, and neither did he. He had just come out of a divorce, and I had been a widow only a short time, not even an entire year had passed yet. We did marry after a few years of living together, if you want to call it a marriage to me it was just superficial. I was definitely out of control; it showed in every aspect of my life. I was no better than the ones that hurt me, and I was sowing some horrible seeds in my life, great seeds of devastation and heartache. I didn't realize it but my son was the one being hurt the most by my lifestyle.

When you are deceived, you are truly blind to the things the enemy has set to destroy you. He sets up things not only to kill you but everything about you and around you. At this time in my life I was in self-destruct mode and my life was spiraling downward in fast motion. I was nowhere near through with this life nor was I ready to quit. There were times that I would go to church and have an experience with God only for it to last a few months. Eventually, my addiction would get the best of me each time and I would be right back in the club. This lifestyle had a huge stronghold on me that would not let go. This truly possessed me and I wanted free but did not stay free. I know that a few people will read this book and know that what I say is true. I can see where God had His hand on me through all of it. I know God goes to the nightclubs too, because if He had not I wouldn't be here today. There is a scripture in Psalms 139 that says: *If I ascend into heaven, You are there; If I make my bed in hell, behold, You are there.* I believe this scripture wholeheartedly because my Lord was right there with me. I cannot tell you how many times I drove home when I could not even remember getting in the car to drive home, much less driving.

A Message With My Mess

During this time in my life, I could not keep a job, nor did I have healthy relationships. My life was one big party after another, and I was a horrible mother. I could not figure out why God saved me and let me live. I was a mess, but I know now God can make a message out of our messes. He is stronger than anything we go through or any demon that is holding us captive. I used to party sometimes every night of the week. There was always a reason to go to the club and have fun. Monday night, there was always a reason; Tuesday night was Beer Bust night at a club. I used to go to The *Club Car*, where you paid $6.00 to get in the door, and then you could drink all the beer you could consume at that price. Wednesday night was ladies' night at most places all over town, so if you were a female, you could drink for half price, which was always a reason for us girls to go. Thursday night was the *"what the hell night!!"*

Friday and Saturday nights were the weekends, so that was a given. Sunday morning, I would sometimes find myself still in the club at the same hour of the day that a lot of people would be at the church praising and worshipping God. Most of the time I was in a club but there were times when I would have keg parties at my house, a party at the lake or out in the woods. There was a place we all used to go way out in the woods and we called it "Camp Catch a Buzz" man, did we ever have a blast out in the woods?

I remember frequently waking up and my head hurting so bad that I could not move. I raised the curtain to look out, and it was a beautiful day, but I could not enjoy it because I was just miserable from all the drinking. Although I had chosen to be married to a man I was not in love with, we weren't faithful to each other. I thought up any excuse I could find to party with my friends; sometimes he would be with me and other times I did not want him anywhere near me. All I wanted to do was drink and party as much as possible on any occasion. However, I did need someone to take care of me and bring money in to pay the bills. I did receive a pretty good sum of money for Chris and me from SSI because I was a widow and Chris was his son. We both received the same monthly amount for as long as he was in school. This ensured that I paid my main bills such as rent, utilities, and car payments. I also worked but never really kept a real job for very long at all. This was who I was or whom I had thought I had become, but I was so deceived, so hurt, and the pain was so deep. I did not realize that the God of the entire universe had His hands of grace and mercy on me. I still had a lot to go through before I came to know this revelation. I had a lot of growing up to do and a lot of things to learn and experience. I drank pretty heavily and experimented some more with marijuana. I stayed in the clubs several nights a week; the worst part was that I left my son for days at a time. I was so busy with my party life that he was not welcome most of the time, and I am so thankful that I had a mother and sister who took care of him for me.

While I was still doing my party life, I also lived with my second husband for about eight years. In some of those years, we had some good times; we bought some land in Pearcy, Arkansas, and I bought a mobile home to put out there. The land had to be cleared, the water well had to be dug, and utilities had to be set up before moving it out there. This was a tremendous amount of work for us, but we got it done and finally the mobile home was ready to be moved and set up on the land. My niece Teresa would come to my house in Pearcy and spend the night with me when my second husband was working. We would watch movies together some would be scary. She would get so scared that she would jump off the couch onto my lap on the scary parts. I would be like you're going to crush me if you do that again. I was just as scared as she was and it didn't help that I lived out in the middle of the woods. She would go with me and my second husband down to the deer woods people called the bottoms in Gurdon many times, and we would set up camp by the riverside. We would build a big campfire at night set under the stars, watch the river as the fish moved around in the water, and listen to the frogs sing. We cooked food by the campfire and washed the pots and pans down by the river. I had so much fun doing this, especially when we had a few beers, wading around in the river and splashing each other till we were soaked.

While Teresa loved going with us to the Gurdon bottoms, she also developed a crush on my ex-husband's friend. I think she would spend time with me just so she could see him because he and his family would also camp out down at Gurdon. She would have loved to have had a relationship with him, but I think he only wanted to be friends. My second husband and I would go down to his Dad's bar called "Whiskers." They had fish, fries, and social gatherings. She would come when they had things outside. She was not allowed in the bar because she was underage.

Whiskers was not a place either one of us should have been at because it was not in a suitable area of town in fact, some people called it skid row. We came here for fun and no matter what occurred, my second husband took care of me.

Moving Forward But Still Stuck

My second husband sometimes doted on me, and I do not think I could have done anything to cause him to get upset with me enough to leave me, so he put up with me through all the hell I put him through. As I think about it, he was not the only one that I hurt in my life. I wounded many people by trying to deal with my hurt. As time passed, we were still continuously enjoying our parties, but my husband was offered a job in New Mexico with one of his logging buddies. I was all game to go out there with him. He told me we could make money out there, and it would be good to get away from Hot Springs for a while. So off we went, dragging my son with me. The town we moved to was Las Vegas in New Mexico, a beautiful, mountainous small town. We lived on a horse ranch there in a small travel trailer. Chris seemed like he liked it there. He got to know the owners of the ranch pretty well and he would spend time at their houses mainly eating. I remember he gained much weight out there because everyone fed him well when he came to their house to play with the other kids, plus he ate at home as well. Las Vegas, New Mexico, is in the foothills of the Rocky Mountains and then it was a tranquil, enchanting little town that felt like you stepped back in time with all the beautiful historic buildings. The area where we lived was out in the country, and you could see the beautiful mountains that enveloped the quaint community. Not a day went by that we didn't take walks or horseback ride up the mountain to see the beautiful scenery.

I remember on one occasion, we went to bed that evening; the weather was wonderful but when we got up the next morning we had thirteen inches of snow. The temperature had dropped that fast everybody said that was normal for this part of the country. All I know is that it was cold. I remember having to put a towel or something at the door because drafty air would come in. When someone would come into the travel trailer then leave that we were staying in, I would say don't forget to put the towel down to keep the draft out. The funny part about this was every time I would say that, my son Chris would run and jump up in a chair and try to hide himself. I finally figured out that he was afraid of the draft; he thought it was a monster or something.

We stayed out in New Mexico for about four months, and of course, when my husband was not working, we would visit some of the pool halls and nightclubs.

This is why I know that when people say that they would do better or things would change if they changed locations, it is just not true. You see, addictive behavior is not geographical; it's a heart issue. I ended up wrecking my beautiful car while I was out in Las Vegas, New Mexico, because I was driving while intoxicated. I didn't hurt anyone or myself I just couldn't get my car fixed because we had no money.

His Fault Not Mine Or So I Thought

My second husband said we would make a lot of money while out there, but that was not true. We had to get food stamps to have something to eat. Our Thanksgiving dinner that year consisted of cheese and crackers. I finally had enough of this lifestyle, especially when my son returned from the ranch house, sounding like he was talking in Spanish. I concluded that if I didn't get out of this place my son would start talking to me in a language I didn't know. So, I packed up my stuff, took a Greyhound bus to the nearest airport 200 miles away in Albuquerque, New Mexico, and then caught a flight home. When I got to the airport, I did not realize that you had to call and make reservations for a flight out, so our flight would not leave until the following day at 6 a.m. My son and I were alone in this big airport and would have to spend the night.

I was afraid and didn't know what to do, so I went to the bathroom and just sat with my child to think. While I was in the bathroom, a few ladies came in, and one started talking to me. I told her about my dilemma she said, "Maybe I can help you. I will be right back, don't go anywhere." She returned and said, "I work for one of the airlines as a flight attendant and we worked it out so that you and your son could sleep in our hospitality suite."

I said, "I have no money for that." The flight attendant said, There is no cost; it's absolutely free. You don't have to worry about anything. We just want you to be safe." She showed me where to go and the suite was beautiful. Not only did I have that beautiful room, but I also had an armed guard outside my door. I believe that was God all the way, without a doubt. I felt bad that morning when I got up and noticed Chris had wet the bed. I got us dressed, tried to clean up what I could, and caught our flight home. This was our first time flying and I was a little apprehensive but we were excited too. We made it to our seats and were buckled in. The plane finally took off. I compare the lift-off to going over a hill in a car and losing your belly. I had this feeling while taking off. Chris looked out the window and said there are ants down there. I looked, and I told him those were cars and buildings. The flight was fun after I overcame my fear; I was glad to be back in Hot Springs, Arkansas, again with my family. After I got back home, my life was back to normal again and I was back to my party scene.

I had so much resentment for my second husband for dragging me out on a get-rich scheme that I blamed him for destroying my car. I used this excuse to have affairs and attend parties. I could go into great detail about each encounter and how I deceived and was deceived by men who had no good intentions for me at all, but the stories are really all the same. Sin is sin and until you finally get enough of it, the sin just keeps getting darker and darker. I lived many years in this lifestyle and did many things that I am not proud of. I delved deep into sin. There were some things I was just too afraid to do. For instance, I know of several people that did some heavy drugs, and they were all around me. It was easy access, but there was always something inside of me that would not let me go that far. Who knows what God really saved me from because if I had delved off into that kind of black hole, I might have never come back out of it. I was more of a drinker than a stoner, although I did a little of that too. I only know that love was on a mission to help me see I could not live in this pain, and I had to stop living in the shadows of sin. I believe God saved me to give me a chance to minister to the hurting and the ones that think they have no other reason to live. I believe God kept His hand on me so I would be alive on planet earth to grab someone out of the darkness and help them run to the light of God's grace.

My second husband and I finally divorced, but we were still seeing each other off and on. I really have no remembrance of marrying this man, nothing special or any great details, I don't even think I have a picture of the occasion. I believe we just went to the justice of the peace and said our I do's. I, however, do remember our divorce. I actually tricked him into agreeing to a divorce because I could get my SSI check back and I told him this would help us because we were struggling financially. I told him I could get my check back, which would help us pay rent and things, and we could just live together after that. I had it all planned out, and it was all about me and nothing was about loving him or any of that; I just wanted what I wanted. I really wanted my cake and to eat it too; I even talked him into taking a job out of state. I told him that when he got everything worked out, I would come to him but I knew I wouldn't I just said this to get him out of the way. I wanted

74

my freedom, but I also wanted to be taken care of and have security. I was a manipulator and an excellent liar. This is what my unresolved pain was doing to me and it was so very sad now that I look back on it all.

Glorious Transformation Tips

Pain Is Not Permanent

Don't let pain have a permanent place in you! Years passed and I battled the unresolved pain not knowing that all I needed to do was just take time and deal with what I felt. Separate the reality from my fears then address each area of my heart that was struggling to move forward.

Chapter Seven

Divine Encounter
with Real Love

This time in my life is when I met the man I am married to now, Larry Jones. He has been my stability and strength, but it didn't start that way. First, I met him in a bar, my niece Teresa and I were driving around one day, and we decided to stop at this little bar and grill that I had been to in the past. We walked in, sat at the bar, and ordered something to drink. During that time, a couple of guys walked in; my niece and I knew one of them because he partied at my house on several occasions. The other guy he was with would come to be my husband one day, but of course, I did not know that at that time, in fact, I actually didn't like him too much; I thought he was somewhat of a jerk. However, there was an element of curiosity about him that I couldn't shake, and I wanted to get to know him better, so I spent some time with him that afternoon. I was supposed to go out with him that night, but my niece and I had to be somewhere else. My niece teased me about him and said some stuff, but I did not take her seriously at all. Anyway, I thought I would never see him again, and that was that. However, God had a different plan, and the very next week, I heard a vehicle pull up in the driveway at my house.

Larry had a very distinct sounding vehicle it was a big red four-wheel-drive Silverado pickup truck with chrome all over it, very beautiful. I told my niece that the guy I met last week was sitting in my driveway right now, and she was just laughing. Larry and I spent lots of time together. He would call me from work and talk to me on his breaks. The minute he left work, he would rush home, get changed, and be at my house. We went out to eat and did some drinking on the weekends. I met his sisters and brothers and loved them instantly. His mother was a bit crusty at the beginning of our relationship, but she warmed up to me after she got to know me better. Larry seemed to be with me and at my house till all hours of the night. I finally asked him to move in with me. It seemed ridiculous that he should stay at my house till two or three in the morning and then go home. So, we moved in together, and that is when everything changed.

Healthy Relationships bring Stability.

My friends did not come over as much, and we did not go out as much as we used to. However, we spent a lot of time at his mother's house. Every Saturday and Sunday, it was the same thing. Sometimes we would go to his sister's house and cook or go to the bar with her and her husband, which was fun. I thought this was what normal couples do, and it was nice. We were stable most of the time, but we still had fun moments on the weekends from time to time.

Larry and I lived together for some time before we married. Honestly, I kept nagging him about it, and he finally gave in. I cannot believe I put up with some of his ways. In the beginning of our relationship, he did not trust me, and he was very possessive and jealous. Sometimes life with him was so miserable that I could not tolerate it and wanted to leave. In fact, one time, I packed up everything and left, the bad thing about it was the mobile home we lived in belonged to me. I thought leaving your own home was bad because you cannot tolerate things anymore. I was tired of being treated like a little child; it was ridiculous because I had to account for every minute I was not with him. If I talked to someone of the opposite sex, I was accused of all sorts of things, and if we went out to the clubs, it was always a fight on the way home.

Life was just miserable, and I thought I would rather be single and wild rather than be captive in a love/hate relationship I hated. Still, I continued to live with him, and we worked some issues out, and things seemed much better after that.

There were things about this man I questioned, but there were some things about him I loved as well. Larry had many wonderful qualities. He was a provider, protector, gave stability, and had a good work ethic. He was honest and hardworking, along with that he was very stern; he did not allow just anything to go on in our home. He was neat and clean and he liked our home to be the same. He liked a hot meal on the table, and his favorite thing was to lay back in the recliner and watch TV. He was mature and reliable; he was satisfied with simple things and did not have to run around all the time getting into a mess. He loved his family, and his mother was precious to him.

There were heartaches that Larry and I have had to endure together throughout our marriage. For the life of me, it seemed that I would lose a loved one in my family, and then he would lose someone. It seemed like it was back and forth for the longest time. My Mother passed away, and then his

Dad passed. He had a sister who died of cancer and left two beautiful children their grandmother raised.

I had a nephew thrown out of a car and run over by a Semi, which was so devastating for my brother and his wife. I lost my son because of drugs and alcohol addictions, and my niece Teresa passed away from either a heart attack or a brain aneurysm. Through all of these tragedies, we hung together, and our marriage grew stronger. God knew who to put me with to help me to endure, and there was no one else that could be my husband. God handpicked him.

I knew this man was my husband. I also knew he loved me, but he had issues of the heart that he needed to heal from just as well as I did. I knew he loved me and he loved my son Chris and he would do anything for us and that was very important to me. However, Chris wanted something very different because I had told him that when my ex-husband moved out, it would be just him and me now. Chris thought he would be the man of the house and he could have his mom all to himself. However, I had a whole different agenda, and I was the type of person who thought she had to have a man around to make her happy. I have learned so much since this time.

Larry had some deep-seated trust issues because of the infidelity in his first marriage. The mistrust he shared with his first wife was fueling the fires of distrust he brought into our relationship. He had every right not to trust me because of how I once lived my life since the tragedy of murder and devastation. I barely trusted myself, but I was determined that I was going to make this relationship work; I did not know why I wanted it to succeed but I knew there was something special about this man, and I needed to dig deeper into him because he had a lot to offer me.

I started working at a printing company that year, 1988, and I worked with a girl that I went to school with; she was always on me that Larry and I should get married. We would be working, and she would start talking about how I could have a June wedding and she would help me with all the details. I was so thrilled I would go home and talk to Larry about it, and he would ask why do you want to mess up a good thing for us. If we were to get married, you would lose your SSI check. Larry was all about the money and working back in those days. He saw no sense in taking a vacation because, as he told me you never get that money or your days back. I thought, oh my God, what have I got myself into? This man does not even want to take a vacation ever! Thank God he began to see things a lot differently and I believe he loves going on vacation more than I do now.

He finally agreed that we should get married, and we started making our wedding arrangements to be in June of that year, which was 1988. It was so fun!

I had my dress and my maid of honor dress handmade. She also did all of my flowers. I bought a few things like our champagne glasses and cake knife with our name and marriage date engraved on them. I also got our guest book, pen and invitations. I loved doing these, it was so outstanding! I was so happy, but Chris was just ok with it; I did not know it then, but a root of rebellion was growing in him like cancer.

We decided that our wedding day would be June 17, 1988, and we had a very simple wedding, nothing fancy as we seemed to argue about every decision. I did a lot of biting my tongue in those days some of my friends and relatives could not understand me but I was so in love with this man and he was so in love with me. I considered his feelings about things because he was important to me and he was good to my son and me. My wedding was held in a little building called the Jaycee Hall, and we decorated it up. We had an open bar with a keg of beer and all kinds of liquor; believe me, I started hitting that keg as soon as I got there that day because I was so nervous! I was so excited that I was finally going to be Mrs. Larry Jones. Oh, how happy I was! The ceremony was simple, my sister was my bridesmaid, and her husband gave me away. We took the weekend off and went to Eureka Springs and Branson. Chris stayed with my mother while we went on our honeymoon; everything was so special. So Larry and I began our life we were happy and got along as long as we kept alcohol out of the equation of our lives. Most of the time we did, but sometimes it got a little rough; somehow, we made it through without killing one another. There was definitely a power higher and stronger than either of us that was pulling for us to make it.

Even today, I look back at all that we have been through and how the odds were stacked against us. I know beyond any doubt that God was with us. God had orchestrated this union, and He made me the wife that Larry needed; The Proverbs 31 woman with a noble character, that was kind, loving, dependable and who would be this man's lifelong companion. God created me to complete and fulfill him. I made a vow that I would understand him like no one else ever could, weep for him when he was hurting, rejoice with him when he was happy, and always be there when he needed someone to care for him.

Together made a vow to accomplish great and mighty things; giving each other joy, strength and provide each other with a purpose for each day. Together we vowed that we would show each other respect and honor and be honest with each other.

We would cherish and be grateful for the moments that we have with each other. The years we spend together and the things we endure together will only make us stronger. Our love only proved to grow deeper with each passing year. There is not one thing that I would have wanted to miss in this relationship. I would not want to miss one thing as we travel together down this road of life with all its twists and turns. We have had sunshine and rain; sometimes, we wanted to give up because our vision for our future together was so unclear. However, I would not have wanted to miss any of the adventures God had laid out for us together.

Glorious Transformation Tips

I belong To God

You are not an orphan. You are not alone. You have not been abandoned. You have been loved and it's time to come face to face with love. I have been set free from the bondages of being a victim of one man's violent crimes. Since I have come to know Jesus. He has shown me how to live life more abundantly. The night of December 31,1976 should have been a time of great celebration. However, because one man decided to take lives it was none of that for me instead it was a night of horror, and shame. However, destiny, mercy and purpose were standing beside me saying, "No you can't have her she is ours!"

Chapter Eight

The Redemptive Power of
God's Unfailing Love and Forgiveness

I praise God every day for His love and forgiveness that was given to me unsparingly by what His Son did on the cross. I am so very thankful for the heritage that I have and the power of a praying family. I am alive and walking with the Lord now because of ALL that some precious members of my family sacrificed to pray for me and not give up. I had a mother and a sister that never let go of the *horns of the altar* and because of their faith, God brought me to my senses and out of the grip of sin. I remember the day well; it was a Sunday morning and for whatever reason I decided to go to a little Pentecostal church that my family attended. The church that I always went to whenever I would take the time out of my drunken days to go to church on Christmas or Easter. I entered the doorway of that little church and the minute I walked past the doorpost, I could feel the love of God engulf me as I had never felt before in my life. I could not contain what I felt, and I began to cry uncontrollably. These people surrounded me and prayed. I cannot remember how I got down to the altar all I know is that I did, and I could feel His presence and it was thick. The very essence of it filled me up and filled the House of God. It was truly amazing. I was filled with His Spirit with the evidence of speaking in tongues, and my life was totally and dramatically changed from that moment forward.

I walked out of that church house changed forever, there is truly none like Him in all the earth and I will love Him forever. I will declare His glory forever and ever; His greatness is beyond all my understanding. I cannot believe how He took a girl that was so messed up and made her as an Oak of Righteousness. I do not always feel like I am that strong, but I know He is bigger than what I feel, and He is larger than all of my misguided conceptions of who I am. If I went by what my mind would tell me about who I am, I would be so misled. I have to believe what His Word says about me and so does every reader of this book. My hope is built on nothing less than Jesus' blood and righteousness, according to his word in the book of Zechariah. His blood paid the price for all my sins and so this is the foundation that I have built my life on.

I would love to tell you that this was my happy ending, and all was wonderful at this point but there were some things that I had to walk through that would shake me to the very core of my being and cause me to question my salvation and everything that I was standing on. I walked out of that church changed, but I would still have to go through some major adjustments to get to where I needed to be. However, I now had the Holy Spirit in my life to help to lead and guide me into what He would have me be, and believe me, this was a process for me it did not take place overnight.

When I got back home and tried to explain to Larry what happened to me, he was happy for me but did not want to hear about it and he sure did not want any of it for himself. That kind of hurt my feelings, and it confused me because I thought surely everybody wants this, but not everyone felt the way I did and so I would walk this way by myself for a while. I was a baby Christian and I would be saved one day and then feel lost the next, but God kept me in the grip of His grace. I remember sharing with my friend Sharon at work and before long she started going back to church. I was so excited because I finally have someone to talk to about God and the Holy Bible. No one at my house really wanted to hear it, so I just kept going to church and living in front of them.

Sharon and I were more like sisters than friends she passed away a few years back and I still miss her so much. I especially miss our morning coffee times when we would share our struggles and what God has been showing us to each other. These were times I cherished so much, and I know there were many days when we would encourage each other with positive words and affirmations to each other. Most days we would end up with both of us crying on each other's shoulders. I can't tell you what a blessing it is to work with someone who loves the Lord and has given their life to him. Sharon was a wonderful and giving friend. Many people came in where we worked, and she would always have a smile or a kind word and if they needed something she would try to meet that need. She loved Larry and me and she wanted us to be happy and she wanted to see Larry come to the Lord as much as I did.

I remember Larry was really partying heavily he would go with his brother just about every weekend. I would go sometimes and just drink coke and sit there and that was pretty boring. It wasn't the same, and I knew I did not need to be in those places. So I decided I would not go anymore, but Larry still went and every time he went, I would turn the praise and worship music on and fall to my knees and worship with my God.

We had mirrors on the wall in our living room that had Budweiser and Miller beer emblems on them I used to think they were so cool. However, now I hated those things being there and so I started praying and God told me to anoint those mirrors with oil and pray that spirit out of my house, and so I did. I not only anointed those mirrors, but I anointed the entire house, everywhere that my husband's sit I anointed. I even anointed his side of the bed, his clothes, his recliner, and I even put anointing oil in his food. He came home and the next day he took every one of those mirrors down off the wall and said he was going to give them to his brother. I was so ecstatic I could hardly contain it!

I wish I could tell you it got better, but it got really worse; I made the devil mad and he raised his ugly head up. Larry seemed to be in a foul mood a lot. He griped at me about going to church; saying there must be some man over there that I was screwing because no one goes or enjoys going to church that much. I kept right on going to church; he made it hard on me every time it seemed like, and he would get mad and accuse me of many things. He got so mad one time that as I was leaving to go to church; he came out the door and threw tea all over my car. That really made me mad, and

I stayed home that day. I thought this is too hard!! I can't handle what I have stirred up.

The next day was a Monday and I went to work and I told my friend what happened and how he accused me of all sorts of things. She encouraged me to keep going and that God would work this all out if I stayed faithful to Him. She invited me to a meeting they were having on Thursday night at the church she went to it was called The Holy Spirit class. I was very interested in the things of the spirit and prophetic gifting and I said yes. She said she had been to some, and she really enjoyed them. So I went, I was very pleased that I went.

The facilitator of that meeting was powerful, and he seemed to know what he was talking about, so I listened intensively to what he had to say. I continued to go to those meetings and I meet some wonderful people and God touched me every time I went. I remember on one occasion I went to the meeting and God touched me so completely and when I got home and I walked through the front door and Larry did a double look at me. The Holy Spirit was all over me and I could feel it, and that look Larry gave me confirmed what I was feeling.

Larry began to treat our home differently, he never brought alcohol into it and he was very careful about using bad words around me. I knew God was working on him I can see my prayers being answered right before my eyes where he was concerned. I remember one night it was New Year's Eve, and he went out with his brother and I went to a Christian singing and when I got home, he wasn't far behind me and it wasn't even midnight yet. I asked him why he came home so early and he said he got sick he asked me if I prayed he would get sick and I laughed to myself and said not today.

God was working so strongly in our lives; he was orchestrating things behind the scenes and bringing my husband to redemption. There was a man that was working with Larry at the time and he had been through a lot. He had lost a child and losing his child made him an alcoholic because of the pain that he carried. I thought I can relate to what he is feeling and I understand how much pain he feels every time he gets up to face another day. This man had found salvation though, and the church that he attended was in revival. He invited Larry and Larry called me and asked me if I wanted to go. God! How could I refuse my husband was asking me to go to church? I did not care what kind of church it was Baptist, Pentecostal, or Assemblies my husband wanted to go to church and I was going!! I was ecstatic. We went, and he dedicated his life to the Lord that night. I couldn't be happier, but it was still a long road to completeness for us. However, this was a splendid start, and I was not about to complain!

Chapter Nine

Moving in a Different Direction

As time went on, we sold our trailer, moved into a quaint little two-bedroom house in town, and Larry would go to church with me here and there. He did not like the church I was attending but my family were going there, and my mother had cancer, for that alone I would not leave her. I had a desire to go with Sharon, my friend, and the woman I worked with to her church because I was still attending the Thursday night meetings and I was also going to a bible study she was having at her house on Tuesday nights. The man that was facilitating the meeting on Tuesday was doing a study on Revelations and he was also a wonderful singer and guitarist. I really enjoyed his acoustic worship he had what I call a Davidic anointing and he would prophecy as he played his guitar. Oh my God, what a wonderful time it was there!! I had never been in this kind of service in my life and it was very refreshing and uplifting.

The Holy Spirit meet with us and it was so thick, I could feel God's presence in both classes they were wonderful and I was learning so much.

I was no longer satisfied with the little church that I was saved in, but I would stay as long as my mother was sick. She enjoyed seeing her kids at Church and I so wanted to please her. However, in reality my heart was somewhere else, but I had to wait until I had that true release from God. Sadly, it was not long before I got the releasement from the little Pentecost church because in October of that year my mother past away. It was a bittersweet time for my siblings and me, in one way I hated to see her take her to leave and go be with her Lord but in another way, it was a blessing because I had seen her suffer enough.

However, she did not suffer as I have seen others do with cancer and taking Chemo treatments. I believe God was very merciful to her and saw that he could use her more effectively if she was with Him. The day she passed away was rainy and cold but the nurse at the hospital that made the rounds that morning had checked on her said she was looking out her hospital window and commented on what a beautiful day it was. She said when she came back to check on her a little later she had passed away; it was quick.

I remember going up to the hospital that day with the rest of my siblings and different friends and family and at that time in my life I was so new to God and everything and I was so sad. I wish I had my mother back but I know beyond a shadow of a doubt where she is and I would not wish her back for anything. I just want to follow her to where she is, just like Ruth followed Naomi to her homeland. I am going to follow my mother to hers.

I recall she had written a letter not long before she passed away and it was addressed to all her kids. My mother may have not been perfect, but she loved her children. I cherish what she left us because it is a holy heritage that has been passed down through the generations of our family. She wrote in this letter the scripture in Psalms 37:25 that says, "I am young and now I am old, yet I have never seen the righteous forsaken or their seed begging bread." This gives me reassurance that I might go through a lot of things in my life, but I have a promise that God would see me through.

I know this to be true that I have never in all my life seen a hungry day and I have never been without clothes to wear. God has made provision for me in so many ways; it is so amazing when I think of it. I can clean my closet out and give what I don't want or need to someone else who needs and it won't be long at all and someone will bless me right back with a hand full of clothes. Even in the days that I was not serving God as I needed to, He always took care of me. I can see His hand of provision in my life and He has always been there for me.

What more could I give my God then to take up my cross and follow Him after all, He has always loved me and engulfed me with that love. I don't doubt His promises because I have seen them come to life in my life so strongly and richly. I have seen His face in so many facets of my life. He has protected me; He has been my Good Shepherd; He has been my Rock and my Buckler, my Shield, He has been my all in all.

So now at this time, my life is taking a new direction some roads will be smooth and full of wonderful adventures with my God. However, other roads will prove treacherous and full of potholes, obstacles, and diversions of hurt and pain that will make me question everything that I am standing on and standing for. God is going to be with me though, so I encourage you to keep reading and find out how sweet His mercies are.

Chapter Ten

Unbridled Rebellion

I wish I could say that my son Chris was having the same things occur in his life as my husband and I were, but this seemed not to be the case. It actually looked like his life was spiraling downhill at very rapid high speed. He was getting in trouble at school, his grades were failing, he was truant a lot, and I would get calls from the principal about him not being at school or getting in trouble at school. He was in complete rebellion against school authority, our authority, and public authority.

Chris had issues when we moved from out of a school district he loved called Lake Hamilton school district into where he used to attend school in kindergarten and first grade. It was actually my old alma mater Lakeside School district where he had bad memories of being bullied by other kids and not treated fairly by teachers. He did not want to move nor could he understand why we had to. He disliked Larry because he was the one pushing us to move. I could understand Larry's complaints about where we lived because the traffic was terrible out that way, especially on Fridays. It would take him about 45 minutes to an hour to get home. When he finally got home, he was really in a foul mood and of course, I was always the first to hear about it and had to put up with his nagging and gripping about us needing to move, so I finally agreed.

The move devastated my son; after that, he fell into a dangerous crowd and started getting into trouble at school and with the law. He was expelled from school for getting into mischief, and finally, he was sent to a summit school. He was in full rebellion and it had to run its course. He and some friends of his finally got into really terrible trouble by getting caught burglarizing a house and he was in jail and went to court. His sentence was probation and restitution, he or should I say I had to pay restitution to the owner of the house they burglarized. You would think this would have taught him, but no, he still got into more trouble. Of course, when you think of it why should he have learned anything from it after all, I was the one paying. If I didn't pay the authorities would take me to jail not him seems all upside down somehow doesn't it?

I remember one particular incident where Chris and some of his friends got the keys to my car and took it one night. I found out later that they did this quite often, he and his friends would pick up the back end of my car and move it out of the way of Larry's truck and then start it and take off with it. Chris did this several times before we realized it, the reason we became aware of is that the sheriff's office called up one night after we had gone to bed and Larry answered the phone and asked us if we knew where our car was.

Larry looked out the door of our mobile home and told the sheriff that it was in the driveway when we went to bed last night. The sheriff said, " I have your son up here at the jail; he is intoxicated and your vehicle is sitting on the edge of Golf Links road. The sheriff told Larry he would need to come to get his son and the car, so he did. I did not go with Larry to pick Chris up from the sheriff's office, but I went with him to get the car.

I was trying to give up smoking at this time in my life and when I woke up to the splendid news that my son had stolen my car that kind of did it for me. I started smoking one cigarette after the other and thinking! I was so mad at him I could have pinched his head off, I was sitting outside on the patio smoking one cigarette after the next when Larry pulled up with him and he got out of the car. He had his head down. He looked up at me as he stepped up on the patio, and I told him to get in the house. I was so mad, and I showed it; I was screaming and hitting at him with everything in me. Larry let me do it for a minute or two, and then I remember him putting his arms around me and saying enough!

I wish I could tell you that this was the last time he took my car or got into any other trouble but it was not; there would be several more times. There was so much rebellion, hurt and pain inside of this child's heart and I realize I help put some of it there by the lifestyle that I lived in front of him. I was not a very good mentor to him for many years; I allowed all kinds of people in his life. I allowed all types of despicable things to go on in front of his innocent little eyes. Party after party in his home, a place that was supposed to be a safe place to him, was a place where on any given night there could be all kinds of people laid out everywhere. I remember him sitting on the keg that was set up in the kitchen pouring beer for everyone. I felt like a real loser and a horrible mother, and I questioned why God let me be the one to live to raise this child because I am doing a horrible job of it.

I have to remember that the reason my child's life was messed up was that I messed my life up. I was trying to get my life better now, but it was going to take some time for these good seeds that I was sowing now to produce a harvest of good crops. I wish I could go back and do things differently but I couldn't the only thing I could do is make the future better. I have made some bad choices in my life and reaped the consequences of those choices; believe me, the reaping has not been pleasant at all. However, I still believe God performs miracles and I believe all things work together for our good.

As I said, there were many more times, my son would get into trouble and this was true. His friends and he would not go to school, he would steal from Larry and me, he would take off and be gone for days at a time and I would never know where he was. I spent many a night crying my eyes out over him, wondering if he was alive or dead. I cried my eyes out and prayed my guts out, it seemed to no avail. He was always in trouble with the law and either drunk or high; I got in every prayer line I could. The devil had a grip on him and it seemed he would not let go. I was devastated and I could find little to no peace. The best peace I had was being in God's presence, where I stayed most of the time.

I remember a couple of incidents when I would be at work and an overcoming feeling would come over me and I could hear a voice in my mind say go home and check your house. I would think I can't do that I am at work. It would keep eating at me so I would let my boss know I had to go home for a little while. I pulled up in the driveway, got out of the car, opened the door and Chris and his friends were at my house having a party.

There was another particular time Chris had been gone a couple of days and I was worried sick and I was praying, asking God to help me. I got a vision of a road with a train track and a little train depot station. I told my sister about the vision and she said she thought she knew where that was and we got in the car and drove to where she thought it was. I went over the railroad tracks, and I looked in my rearview mirror and there was Chris and his friend sitting on a bench. The Holy Spirit knew exactly where he was and took me to him. I am so thankful for the gifts of the spirit and discernment.

My church family at this time helped me through some troublesome times, I seemed to be an emotional wreck at times. However, I had not seen the worse of this vile disease called addiction yet. Chris was at the worst time of his life, the powers of the drugs that held him in bondage drove him. I know that he was doing several street drugs which comprised marijuana, crack cocaine, hash, alcohol etc… I know he used drugs in many forms and ways, he mostly smoked but also shot up. He was sickly looking, very thin and would not practice good hygiene.

He would be gone from home days at a time and then one day he would call and tell me he was hungry and would I please come and get him. Of course, I would I would have to lecture him and all. He had already stopped going to school, so I quit trying to even talk to him about that. However, he tried to get his GED but never finished the classes it took to get it. Also, he tried to get his driver's license and I think he passed the test but he got them taken away from him. There were times I thought he was trying to do better and I could almost see a glimmer of hope, he even met a nice girl and I thought he and her were planning on getting married and starting a life together.

However, life circumstances took a turn for the worse and Chris died tragically one Monday night in October of 1994. I remember the night that Larry woke me up early on the morning of the 19th of October 1994 and told me to get up, that Lena and her mother were on their way over to talk to me about what had happened last night. About that time the doorbell rang, and it was then Lena began to tell me what happened. She broke down and her mother finished the story. I could not understand what they were trying to tell me at first but I finally wrapped my head around the fact that my son was dead.

I was having trouble comprehending how this happened; I thought one thing but it was actually something else entirely. Actually, it took me a few days to understand how he really died and that they found him dead in a Federal Express Dropbox. I thought they were telling me he got caught in a conveyer belt at the UPS store. I did not understand this at all; it was like my mind was in a fog.

The things that transpired leading up to this were uncanny when I think about them. One incident was I had been reading a book by an author *Barbara Johnson* and in this book she had prayed for her son to come out of a homosexual lifestyle. She had a vision of wrapping her son up in a box and taking him up to the Throne of God and giving her son as a gift to God. As she ascended back down the stairs from God's throne she looked back over her shoulder and God was opening her gift and was playing with and holding her son like he was a baby. I thought I want to do that because if this worked for her it should work for me because God is no respecter of persons what he does for one, he can do for another. If her son came out of the gay lifestyle, then my son can be delivered from addictions. I was so desperate I would try anything, so I envisioned me wrapping my son up in a box and taking him to the throne of God and giving him as a gift to God. Little did I know they would find him in a box.

I blamed myself for this for the longest! I believed I may have caused his death by praying that way. I know now that this was not right thinking and if there was anything to this, I was thankful that God accepted my son as my gift and now he is in heaven with Him.

Another incident happened when I saw Chris's picture in the newspaper in The Most Wanted in Hot Springs section. This broke my heart, the day I saw it this was Wednesday night, and I went to church that night. When I got to church, I went to the back and I passed by the sound booth where my pastor's wife was and she asked me if I was alright that she had seen the paper. I told her no, and that I was so heartbroken to see that, she asked me if I wanted them to pray for me and I said yes.

Different ones gathered around me, and I remember falling out in the Spirit and crying so hard. My heart hurt so badly that I thought I would have a heart attack right then and there. One of the people praying for me laid their hand on my heart and started praying for my heart. Immediately I felt that pain subside, they got through praying for me and I stood up. One woman that is a great friend of mine and is an awesome prayer warrior went and got her bible and come over to me and said God wants you to see something. She opened her bible to Isaiah chapter 22:23 which says, "And I will fasten him as a nail in a sure place, and he shall be for a glorious throne to his father's house." I was taken aback by this because this is the scripture that God gave me concerning Chris. I told her what happened and how Chris was Most Wanted in Hot Springs. I admitted that seeing that broke my heart because the picture didn't even look like him. It was a mug shot of when he was on drugs really bad and he was very thin. She began to get all excited, and she said, well He is most wanted by the Holy Ghost! This so encouraged me to the point that I was crying and praising God with all that was in me.

Chapter Eleven

What Were They Trying to Tell Me

I absolutely did not know what to do with this new information about my son; I could not believe that this just transpired in my life! This did not seem real; it was like it was dreamlike, almost bizarre. My heart felt like someone had reached into my chest, grabbed it, squeezed it, pulled it out and then showed it to me. The first person I remember around me at the wee hours of that morning when all this transpired was our pastor at that time. He was very comforting and a familiar face, which was very encouraging. I was sure he could help me understand what was really going on. I always had a lot of confidence in this man; he is probably one of the most knowledgeable men about the things of God that I would ever know. So I felt very good in his presence and knew I would be alright in my heart.

My understanding of what had just transpired was very unclear, and I needed someone to help me gain insight into what was happening. I knew this man who was our pastor could help me; and he tried to help me as best he could. However, I was a total mess, and I did not how to take this news. I remember being in my bedroom and the radio alarm went off, and it was playing the praise song, *"It is well with my soul.* "I screamed to the top of my lungs and shouted out No!! My husband and our Pastor came running back; I was on the floor crawling around like a madwoman!! I was trying to crawl to the radio alarm clock to turn it off and I could not seem to get there! I was trying to silence what was coming out of the radio with my screams! I could not stand the thought of what it was saying because my soul knew what the words were trying to tell me and I did not want to hear those words! Believe me they are some of the most beloved words to me now, but at this time I could not bear to hear that it was well with my son's soul because this was telling me what I did not want to hear.

My pastor prayed for me, and I finally found comfort in his prayers. I finally came out of the bedroom and I sat on the couch right beside that man of God and he held me and I cried and I cried. I did not know if I would ever be the same emotionally again or not. I later determined that I would never be the same emotionally, spiritually, or physically.

My life was now forever altered across the pages of my history; I would again have to find a new normal for my life.

As the wee hours of daybreak gave in to the early hours of sunup, the household seemed like it held an odd feeling of vagueness or uncertainty. I recall sitting at the kitchen table looking into the cup of coffee that someone had poured for me. For the life of me, the coffee seemed to have a blacker than normal look as I sat there and swirled it with my spoon and put creamer in to try and take the black of this horrible night's effects away. However, it was to no avail.

I sat and just looked at what the night had offered to me once again, and I could make sense of nothing that had transpired. I knew my son would walk through the door any moment and all of this would have been a huge mistake. I did not want to believe any of this, and I wasn't going to, and I sure didn't have to. Anyway, no one was explaining it to me and not understanding it all was very frustrating. My baby sister lived with Larry and me at the time and she seemed to be constantly on the phone telling everyone the same thing that the people had been telling us earlier. I wondered why she should be doing this when she was not sure about anything either. I was trying to make some sense out of all this, and I was having a huge problem comprehending what had happened to my son.

My understanding was so unclear, and I could not figure out how my son got caught on a conveyor belt or whatever at UPS. However, I found out later that this is far from what really happened, it was actually a Federal Express Drop Box that my son was caught in and could not get out of. I could not imagine this and I tried but I could not wrap my head around the image of this or the fact that the *Jaws of Life* cut him out of this box. This was a very bizarre accident to say the least, I could not even imagine what a Fed Ex box looked like, and at a later time someone took me to look at one. After I saw it I was still taken back by this contraption because someone had to help him get in this box, it was not something you could do by yourself.

People and family started showing up at my house, the first person I recall being there was my older sister and her family, and she was so distraught. Her family entered the house and she was crying and crying, not believing what she had heard. She always had a special place for my son in her heart. She had helped me raise Chris when his daddy died years prior and she took care of him many nights while I was in my rebellion and hurt. She told me one night that Chris would watch out the window and wonder when his momma was going to come home and be with him. This was ironic because this was exactly what I was thinking, only I was wondering when Chris would come home to me. I remember keeping my eye on the door and constantly looking out the window for any odd car he might pull up in.

There were so many unanswered questions rolling over in my mind and I was so fortunate that I had my husband as a huge support system for me right now because I could not have done the things that needed to be done on this day or the next few days ahead. This was only the beginning of sorrows and I was not coping through it very well at all.

Glorious Transformation Tips

Holy Spirit Changed My Whole Life

God wants you and he chose you for more. I cannot remember how I got down to the altar all I know is that I did, and I could feel His presence and it was thick. The very essence of it filled me up and filled the House of God. It was truly amazing. I was filled with His Spirit with the evidence of speaking in tongues, and my life was totally and dramatically changed from that moment forward.

Chapter Twelve

Trying to put the
Shattered Pieces back Together

I guess after the initial shock of everything, I felt a lot like Humpty Dumpty. My life had spiraled way out of control, and I felt so broken inside and out. I needed God to help me in some way, but I did not know how to reach out to Him. I really did not know if I wanted to reach out to a God that would allow such a thing to transpire. My understanding was so unclear, and I just wanted this awfulness to be over with so that I could get back to normal. I heard someone say once that normal is just a setting on your dryer and as I look back on my life, I believe that this is true. Deep down deep inside, I knew my life would never be normal again. My world has been rocked to my core on a couple of occasions and I do not know how I have stood in the hard places but somehow, I have withstood those tough places and through it all I have learned to trust Jesus even more.

The days ahead were very hard there was the funeral and people in and out and trying to be pleasant, when all I wanted to do was crawl in a hole somewhere and die. My husband took care of all the funeral arrangements; the only thing I decided on was the casket. He took me to the funeral home and I remember walking into the room where all the caskets were. I hated this but knew it had to be done so I walked around the room several times and finally decided on a beautiful blue one with etchings on the sides of angels. One of the hardest things I had to do was pick out a casket to put my baby in; this should never be done because it is so unnatural. The casket was beautiful, but today, as I sit here writing this, I can't remember much about it, only that it holds my son's remains. The day of the funeral I remember getting to the church, I have no idea who rode with me or what the conversation was that morning. All I know is when they opened the church door and escorted me up to the front where the family section was, it seemed so unreal. I felt like I was in a movie and watching it from somewhere far, far away.

The ushers set me down and as I begin to sit down, I looked over at the other side where Chris's friends and the families' friends were seated and the church was completely full. Most of the guys that Chris ran around with were all there, his cousins and close family members. I remember there was not a dry eye in the house and it occurred to me how much everyone loved my son. I hoped he was somewhere seeing all of this too. I remember watching those boys who were the pallbearers and how they could barely keep still because their emotions were so strong through the service. As I sit and reminisce about it now, I believe there should have been an altar call that day because I believe they all would have flooded the altar.

After the funeral the first few days were full of people in and out of our house. People wanted to do so much for me. The church my husband and I were a part of at that time enveloped us with so much love. We had plenty to eat, my home was taken care of and so were we. I could never thank them enough for all they did for us. I love them to this day and I will always have a special bond with them for how they took care of us in our time of great need. I fought much emotional trauma the days after the funeral, it was hard for me to sleep or relax. By this time friends and family were not coming around as much and the house was quiet. I would let my emotions and imagination run away with me. I had so much on my mind and so many emotions, I guess I needed some therapy but I did not know about that kind of thing in those days. I did not know that I was suffering from PTSD all I knew is that I was hurting inside so much. I would wake up in the middle of the night and be so afraid for no reason! I remember being terrified that something bad would happen and I could do nothing to stop it! I would look out the windows of my home into the total darkness and horrible thoughts would come rushing to the front of my mind! I would be afraid to let my dog out to play outside because I thought he would get killed or run over by a car. I was scared that my husband was going to get killed on the job, or get in a car wreck going or coming to work. I was so anxious about everything it was complete and total bondage!

Every emotion that could be felt I felt it. It was like my emotions were running amuck and I had no way to stop the feelings! I felt tremendous guilt and pain because I thought I should have and could have done something to make this not happen in the first place. I thought that if I had been a better mother, none of this would have happened, and it is all my fault because I was such a bad person in my past life!! I felt like I was going absolutely crazy and had no way to stop this!! I needed some serious therapy or counseling!! So what do you think I did to try and stop the voices, I added insult to injury by getting intoxicated as I could, which was no help at all! It only made things worse so now I had that to deal with as well! Humans are so stupid sometimes, we run to the very thing that we should be running away from in life.

Larry had gone to the deer camp and was going to be gone a week and this gave me the opportunity I needed to deal with the pain the way I wanted to. I told my sister who was living with us at the time that I wanted to go and get as drunk as possible. Of course, she was all on board for it so we went and got with some friends and I drank all the alcohol I could that night without killing myself. I think I truly wanted to kill myself by drinking myself to death but that didn't happen. I just got a huge headache and had a tantrum in front of my sister and God. I started kicking, screaming, and hollering to the top of my lungs and then I had a good cry.

Larry came home early from deer camp. He said, "The Lord spoke to me about what you were doing, and I needed to come home." I was very thankful really that God cared that much for me, my marriage, and my life. I felt so bad about what I had done. I guess I just needed to vent and I kind of got amnesia about the good things my God had done for me, and I resorted back to old behaviors. Sometimes it is so easy to forget but amnesia will kill you if you let it. There is one thing I never want to forget: God's goodness is new every morning and he has a whole new batched cooked up every day for us.

I was trying very hard to put the shattered pieces of my life back together again; the tragedy was so overwhelming that I thought how can this be real? I knew my son would walk through the front door any minute and life would resume once again. This was just an awful nightmare and I was going to wake up and it is going to be over, but sadly this was not the truth. The truth was my son was never coming home and life would never be the same again. My life has been forever altered like a piece of fabric cut the wrong way and is good for nothing, at least that's what I thought.

I remember getting an invitation to a meeting for parents whose children no longer lived. My sister and I went to it. I needed help so badly and was willing to try anything because I knew my old lifestyle habits would not fix this. I found out that this meeting was not what I needed; some of the parents were still in much grief and their children had been deceased for ten or more years. I thought, oh my God I do not want to suffer as long as they have. I have to find peace with this soon. I have to find some way to cope with what has happened to me. I needed the Holy Spirit to touch me and heal me because I was suffering so badly on the inside. I felt like my insides were torn out and bleeding to death.

My sister and I left the meeting and I felt nothing yet still needed something! Well, it just so happened that there was a Women's Aglow meeting that night and I knew it had already started. It had been going on for about an hour, but I still had this overwhelming drawing to go. I asked my sister if she wanted to go or if she minded if we went up there and she didn't care that we could go. So we went, we walked into the meeting and sat on the back row, the meeting, of course, was already in progress so we tried to be as quiet as possible.

A little black woman was speaking that night and she was doing a really good job although I cannot tell you anything that she was preaching on. I was just listening to her and all of the sudden she stopped in the middle of her sermon and she looked back at me and said come up here, honey. I wasn't sure if she really meant me but deep down I knew God was calling to me. She asked me again and said, " Yes, you honey come up here, I began to walk up to the front and the closer I got to her, the more I could feel the anointing of Almighty God!! She asked me she said you love the lord don't you and I shook my head yes. She said, you have been through devastation haven't you and I began to cry. I knew this was the Holy Spirit speaking through her to me. She continued and said the Lord wants you to know that He has seen it all and will avenge you.

I began to cry so hard and so loud it came from down deep within me. My feet fell out from under me and all those women came and gathered around me and began ministering to me. I cannot tell you what a release that was. I received so much healing that night and my life was different after I walked out of that meeting. I cannot tell you what else happened in that meeting that night except that I did walk up to that lady that I had never laid eyes on before and thanked her for being obedient to God. I told her a little of what I had been through and she held me and hugged me for the longest time.

After this wonderful encounter with the Holy Spirit, my journey to wholeness began. I found that the Word of God meant a lot more to me than it ever had before and that the Christian songs I listened to before had new meanings with every word I heard. I listened to many different preachers and read many books to learn how to cope with all the devastation I had been through. I wish I could tell you that I never stumbled, doubted or fell but that would be a lie however every time I have struggled, I have become stronger because my God has been with me to help and encourage me. I had times when I just went through the motions and did not really feel anything.

I just do what I think is the right thing to do and I keep persevering until I find stability.

My son would be turning forty-eight this year if he was still alive and it seems farfetched that he has been gone from us for twenty-seven years now. However, I have to look at it in a different perspective to be able to cope with things. I always say he is twenty-eight years old in heaven right now and when I say that it puts a smile on my face and everyone else's face too. He has experienced things in the Heavenly realm that we on planet earth no nothing about. My heart hurts so badly sometimes because I miss him desperately but I know where he is and one day when my journey on earth is done, I will see him again and it will be a wonderful reunion as we gather with family members who are in heaven. I am looking forward to a great time when all our troubles are over and we sit down together for that great marriage supper of the Lamb. Hallelujah!! The King is coming and we will be reunited with the Heavenly Host!! There will be no more sickness, no more tragedy, no more shame and no more heartache or pain!!

Praise God!! Maranatha Lord Jesus!!

Conclusion

J erry Don died in the prison he was incarcerated in since the night of his capture or should I say early hours of January 1, 1977. He tried several times to get clemency for his crimes, but he never could gain that freedom he sought so desperately. I on the other hand have been set free from my bondages of being a victim of one man's violent crimes. Since I have come to know Jesus and lived for Him He has shown me how to live life more abundantly

The night of December 31, 1976 should have been a time of great celebration, a time to make New Year's resolutions together. A time to toast champagne and kiss the one you love at the stroke of midnight. However, because one man decided to take lives it was none of that for me instead it was a night of horror, a night of shame, and a night that should have never been. However, destiny was there with me, mercy and purpose were standing beside me saying, "No you can't have her she is ours!" They looked straight in the eyes of death and said," Death you have to move back you have no hold on her you must set her free!"

I know this now more than I know anything else. God was with me through the entire ordeal, I should have died that night, but God had another plan for my life. An assassin bullet could not take me out, insanity could not rob me and it should have, and shame could not keep me. I have a new life now but it took quite a bit to get there. I wish I could tell you that I never had to endure anything else after this, but that is not true. I have suffered many things and I have lost more than I ever cared to give up.

However, through it, all God has shown Himself to be my Refuge, my High Tower, my Stronghold, my Peace, and my Comfort. I could never have made it through the places I have been without His hand guiding me and His Spirit comforting me. I do not have answers to the questions that arise in my spirit from time to time. I cannot explain away the reasons I had to be a victim of a violent crime. All I know is that God brought me through it, and I am no longer a victim of anything but I am victorious through Christ who gave me the strength to endure such horrors. I have no doubt that Christ has been with me all my life through every situation through being molested as a child, trying to mask my pain with drugs and alcohol and losing my son so tragically because of his own struggle with drugs and alcohol.

I pray for understanding every day and sometimes God will give me a reassuring word or He will just bless me in unimaginable ways. My life is forever hidden in God and I trust that he will take care of me and use me to bring his glory to Earth. If my story will help someone else, I want to share it as often as he requires me to. I hope this touches the lives and hearts of all who read it. It is part of my life spilled out as a drink offering to those who are struggling with the cares of their own lives.

Please be encouraged that if you have been a victim of a violent crime or have endured something in your life that you feel is unbearable, know there is help and healing for you through Jesus Christ. He is here for you and He will help you in your darkest hour of despair. Remember God is a restorer of paths to dwell in and He will give back to you what the enemy has stolen. I know this because God has restored to me some things that I thought I would never get back in my life. Here are some examples: He restored my education, I quit school in the tenth grade and now I have

126

earned a bachelor's degree in Psychology. God has given me teaching abilities to be able to give hurting people tools they can use to defeat the enemies in their life and destroy strongholds. God restored me to be a Mother which I thought would never happen since Chris was my only son. However, God has given me many spiritual sons and daughters and I am so proud that I can know this kind of love.

I cannot bring my son back but praise God I know where he is and God is keeping my glorious treasure like a nail in a sure place and when it is time I will be with him again. I hope my story has brought some healing to you as you have read the pages of my pain. Thank you very much for spending some time with me as I shared my scars with you. I don't begrudge the scars but I thank God for my scars because they have made me love my God and others more than I could imagine. I pray that God would richly bless you and keep you in the grip of his grace as he did me as I was tested and tried but came through victorious in the end as I walked through the fires of adversity and survived this double devastation.

Glorious Transformation Tips

My Scars

Be thankful for your scars. Thank you very much for spending some time with me as I shared my scars with you. I don't begrudge the scars but I thank God for my scars because they have made me love my God and others more than I could imagine.

The End Matter

Where I am now

I still have my mind, I still love the Lord and I am alive and well living in my retirement years. I just recently retired from my job and am looking for something to keep me from being too bored. I would like to use this book as a ministry tool to help others with tragedy, grief, and trauma that they have experienced in life. If the Lord opens the doors would like to go places and share my testimony with others as God allows.

There are several scripture verses that I have stood on since going through the sufferings and tragedies of my life.

- *Psalms 91: 4-6 He will cover you with His pinions and under His wings, you will find refuge; His faithfulness is a shield and buckler. You will not fear the terror of the night, nor the arrow*

that flies by day, nor the pestilence that stalks in the darkness
that wastes at noonday.

- *Isaiah 41:10 Fear not, for I am with you, be not dismayed, for I am your God; I will strengthen you, I will help you, I will uphold you with my righteous right hand.*
- *Psalms 34:18 The Lord is close to the brokenhearted, He rescues those whose spirits are crushed*
- *Psalms 147:3 He heals the brokenhearted and bandages their wounds.*
- *Deuteronomy 31:6 The Lord your God will go with you. He will not leave you or forget you*
- *Isaiah 30:15 In quietness and confidence shall be your strength.*
- *Isaiah 40:29 He gives strength to the weary and increases the power of the weak.*
- *Isaiah 54:10 For the mountains may depart and the hills be removed but my steadfast love shall not depart from you.*
- *Isaiah 61:1 The Spirit of the Sovereign Lord is on me because the Lord has anointed me to proclaim good news to the poor, He has sent me to bind up the brokenhearted, to proclaim freedom for the captives and release from darkness for the prisoners.*

Here are a few scriptures I would probably have to write the whole bible because they are all my favorites. Finally, as I have lived for the Lord these many years, I have discovered that what God starts all of Hell cannot defeat. I had a destiny and the enemy tried to take me out long before my time so that I would not be able to finish my race and achieve my goal. I know the devil is a liar and he failed in his attempt to stop what God had ordained in me. I stand with my armor on and I belong to God. I will not set back and let the devil win and I will not be stopped. There is a double portion anointing within me and I want to go forward for a greater influence. I pray my praise will be louder than my pain. There is a generation that I want to build up with my story and I thank God that I can speak into the destiny of others and bring hope and peace.

Be Encouraged

God created me with a purpose and the very fact that I am alive lets me know that. If the enemy had his way I would have died as a child or a young adult without knowing Christ at a time when I had no idea who I was or what I was supposed to do. I was made by God and for God. He has a long-range plan for my life to get this book out and to be able to share my story with whoever needs it. I pray that I can help a multitude of people by letting my scars show through the pages of this book. God planned me for His pleasure, and I went through everything I did for His pleasure and His purpose. He planned all of this to shower His love on me through all the horrible things that I went through. Another revelation that I am quite aware of is that His hand was upon me as I went through all of it and guess what His hand is upon you too. He knows what you have been through as well.

Long before God created the universe He had me and you in mind. He loves us and He wants us to love Him back. God loves us in spite of everything we have done or will ever do. God wants us to lay down all these things we have been through even though some are very hurtful and love Him with all our hearts. I hope that the words through this book have spoken to that place that has been so bruised and wounded so that you can walk in victory. When you go through certain things that devastate your life, they are often called traumas. This event or incident has devastated your soul and it stays with you for a long time. Some traumas linger and last a long time like child abuse, which triggers things within us.

Triggers do not come so you can prepare for them. You may smell a certain smell or you will hear a certain sound and it will bring back a remembrance to you instantly; this is a trigger. The sound or smell brings back something you went through a long time ago and devastated your soul. There is a way you can overcome triggers and that is by realizing that you have gone through enough. When you begin to realize this, you can then triumph because you get a revelation that you are still here and the enemy didn't take you out through all the trauma you went through by realizing that you have gone through enough. You begin to triumph by realizing that you are still here. The enemy didn't take you out through the trauma. You realize with excitement that you made it through, you wear a crown of victory and you have come full circle through your trauma and pain.

We have to rethink how we handle traumatic experiences within our lives. Trauma is an experience of feeling weighed down or paralyzed by some kind of experience in your life such as rejection, the death of a loved one, a sadistic disaster or a victim of a violent crime. A wicked person can traumatize you with their trauma; it happened to me when I was nineteen. People make evil choices in their life and that choice affects others in devastating ways the way that it affected me. God will reprimand evil one day, but we have the right to choose and so do others.

People choose to do wrong and to do things against God's law but we have to know that God loves us through others' choices. Sin brought suffering into the world and the world is broken because of sin. People do things that will break your heart and hurt you. The world is not heaven and nothing works properly here. Sin and evil cause pain and

God grieves when He sees His children hurting from other people's choices. *Isaiah 63:9 says that God suffers with you He sees your suffering, and God has emotion and He hurts when His children suffer. Psalms 55:8 God keeps a record of all our sorrows and He collects all your tears and they are written in His book.*

This scripture tells us how much God feels our pain, that He cares and we serve a suffering God. God weeps with what makes you weep and God will judge evil one day. God will bring good out of bad if we will but trust him, after all He had a plan for His son Jesus when he hung on the cross and died. God knew that His son Jesus rose on the third day completely victorious. So, if you trust Him He will turn your trauma and abuse into a glorious transformation. As I close this book I ask you to look at the suffering that you have endured and begin to thank God that you made it through this devastation.

My Prayers For You

I pray for you to forgive those that you need to and know that people make choices that are not always good. Ask yourself if there is anything within you or a choice that you have made that maybe you have regrets about. I know I have had many things to lay before the Lord and ask His forgiveness for. I pray that you would realize that God loves you and He feels your pain, He had to watch while the world crucified His Son. I pray that you would begin to see yourself as God sees you. Understand that He has called you from the foundation of the earth and marked you as His Child by the Holy Spirit. You cannot be loved more than you are right at this very moment. May God bless you and keep you and let His face shine upon you and give you hope.

Glorious Transformation Tips

Memories Live On

Memories of our lives, of our works and our deeds will continue in others." When someone leaves, they aren't gone far. I have learned that they rest in my arms right there in my heart.

After Thoughts and Fond Memories

My Mother

I have very fond memories of several people in my family but the one that stands out the most is my mother. She was a simple woman who loved the Lord with all her heart. She wanted the best for her children; she sacrificed many things for the benefit of her children. I don't believe that it was a coincidence that I was placed in this woman's womb. I believe God put me there so she could be my mother; it was God ordained from the foundations of the earth.

My Mother was happy when her children were happy; when they were sad she was sad as well. When they were scared, she would protect them. Some people called her overprotective and I believe she was but she loved her children with an undying love. She would never want any harm to come to any one of them. She was one of the strongest women that I know she endured so many things and I believe that I get my strength from my mother. My mother wanted the best for her children she wanted them to succeed in life. She wanted us to fulfill our purpose and passions. There is a letter that she wrote and left us, kids, before she passed away and it said:

I put my trust in God, as my parents and grandparents before us. I pray for my children all to be saved.

My great grandparents all were saved. My forefathers were Holy Spirit-filled people. Great grandfather John Kelly for one and my great grandmother Mat Kelly.

In our bible, it says to put our trust in God. King David himself said he had never seen a righteous man begging. Delight yourself in God; He will take care of you. Praise to our God forever. Glory to the Everlasting King Christ Jesus. See my Mother in glory.

I treasure this letter and as I reflect on it now it makes me cry and feel proud that I have such a Godly heritage that I had ancestors before me that served God and knew how to pray. I believe there were people in my family lineage that interceded for the generations to come, and I believe I am part of that generation.

The book of Isaiah chapter 40 says that the grass withers the flowers fade but the Word of God will stand forever. We are like the grass of the field; it is here today and gone tomorrow but one thing we can be sure of is that if God has spoken a word to you it will stand forever and you never need to doubt that. I know God spoke to my Mother those words to leave her children and I receive those words into my spirit and pray that God will bring the increase of those precious words.

My Father

I don't have any memories of my Father but I do have what people mainly siblings have told me about this man. I was very young when he passed away young enough not to remember. I know that he was a good man and a hard worker. He loved his home and family, he took care of his family with a stern and loving hand. He loved to garden, he raised farm animals, and he loved home-cooked meals. I was told that he left home when he was only six years old, and this is when he started being a Golf Caddie for Golfers at the Country Club. Some of the men he caddied for were said to be very influential,l and he would even be a caretaker of the homes these men owned in Hot Springs when they were away. He served his country well in the military, and there are many places in my hometown where you can still see his handiwork as a bricklayer and a cement finisher. He loved sitting out on the porch and enjoying a good pipe or a cigarette after his meals.

On occasion, my Father would take me to the store and get me something special just because he was always thinking about his children. I was told that my father was sick with Leukemia and hardening of the arteries he stayed in the VA hospital for a time, where he received surgery and treatments for these diseases. He died around my birthday in 1961, my older brother was with him downtown close to the train depot when he had a cerebral hemorrhage and later died at a hospital in town. I wish I knew more about my real father than what I do. I sometimes feel cheated because God took him when I was so young.

My Siblings

I have several siblings that have brought me much joy throughout the years. My oldest sister, however, died when she was fairly young with cancer. Her children were devastated. I have lost contact with one of them throughout the years but the other I stay in touch with them through social media. I am happy that I can do that. Cancer took her very fast; she was diagnosed in October of that year and passed away in January of the next year. She came and spent some time with us here in Hot Springs the summer before she got sick, and we celebrated her birthday and had a great time while she was here.

I remember visiting her from time to time as well when she lived out in the country. She could grow beautiful flowers and could maintain a garden fantastically. She had some of the most beautiful crops from her endeavors; I believe that she grew the most beautiful heads of lettuce and tomatoes I have ever seen. She loved the simple life and gave herself to that kind of living, and it was glorious when I would visit with her. I remember on one occasion that it was not so wonderful, though because she made us an amazing supper of fried deer meat, fried potatoes, and big cat head homemade biscuits which were so good. I say it was not so wonderful because as I was biting down on a piece of the deer meat, there was sudden excruciating pain in my mouth. I immediately spit out the morsels and there was a round pellet that came from a gun of some kind. I was in so much pain for the rest of my stay at her house, and when I got back home, I had to go to the dentist and get my tooth fixed. I would have done it all over again to gain the experiences that I had staying with her on her farm and getting to fish from her ponds. The time I spent with her was always an exciting experience that I would not soon forget.

My other older sister is the one I am closest to; she has always been a huge part of my life. I have never lost contact with her, and I call her during the week to check on her and just to her sweet voice. She has suffered so much from physical illnesses, but God has seen her through her infirmities. She has suffered so many infirmities in her body, some of which should have taken her out, but God was merciful and brought her through. She had tuberculosis as a child and cervical cancer when she was twenty-eight. She had open heart surgery when she was in her 30's because of her heart and artery disease that she still battles today. She had stage 4 breast cancer and had to have one breast removed and underwent several chemotherapy treatments when she was sixty. She was miraculously healed by the power of God and was not given any hope by doctors, but God raised her up from this awful disease. Some years late,r she had a stroke that left her crippled in her body, but she has gotten better and can walk with the aid of a cane. She has breathing problems because of COPD and has to take breathing treatments several times a day.

With all the physical ailments and diseases that she has endured, she has remained faithful to her God and God has been faithful to her. She has suffered the loss of a child as well. She lost my niece Teresa to a brain aneurysm at the young age of thirty-five. The hospital she was taken to was not equipped to treat her effectively, but they tried to resuscitate her but were unsuccessful. This was a great loss for our family, and I remember grieving so hard I thought I would have a heart attack myself. I have two brothers, one older and one younger brother my older brother went into the military when he was young and served in the Vietnam War. I remember my mother praying for him many nights as she lay awake in her bed, calling out to God to keep His hand on her son and bring him back home. God honored her wishes and brought him home, but he was wounded in battle and received the Purple Heart.

My older brother came to know the Lord, and he serves the Lord with all his heart. He will get up early in the morning and pray for his family and anyone that God puts on his heart. He has also had a lot of physical ailments and diseases that he has had to fight in his body. He had open heart surgery as well and came through that and has to be treated with medication but he has overcome a lot of this disease. He, too, lost a child his only son as I did; his death was very tragic and devastated the family. It was an automobile accident, the kids were coming home from a church function when the driver fell asleep at the wheel, and my brother's son was thrown from the car into the path of a semi-truck. The boy was in the backseat of the car, sleeping, when this accident happened. We pray God was merciful and he escaped any pain. The family could not see him at the funeral. It was a closed casket because of his injuries. My brother and his precious wife have never had complete closure from this devastating tragedy.

My younger brother was into drugs and alcohol for a time. The devil tried to take him out and almost succeeded, but God rescued him from that lifestyle. Several years later, he met the woman God had for him from the foundations of the earth. They married and had five children. He has a close relationship with his God, and his kids are all almost grown now. I have two twin sisters that were born of my sixth birthday. What a birthday present. My mother got out easy doing it this way I guess because there is one day to celebrate three birthdays instead of three different days. She also saved herself with only having to do one cake and put three names on it. This was pretty ingenious if you ask me; she was a very smart lady. I am sure God also had a hand in this, so I thank him for my sisters. These girls are not identical, but what you call fraternal twins meaning they don't look alike. I think they are very much different but the same. They are both of tender hearts and are very passionate about things and the people they love.

One is a nurse; she has a huge heart for people, so I believe God put her in the right occupation because she not only has healing in her hands but also has healing in her words to minister to the people that she has under her care. The other sister is one that is a wiz with numbers. She is my go-to person when I have questions about tax or accounting. She is the one who helped me with making through all my Algebra classes through getting my degree. My sister who is the nurse has a very sensitive heart. She works with heart patients and has been a huge help to my relatives and friends who have had heart problems. You have to be careful with her though because she wants you to have the best treatment you can get so she will go behind the scenes and talk to whomever she needs to and get you help. She has a beautiful daughter and a gorgeous grandbaby that she loves with all her heart. My other sister, the Math whiz, is very tender-hearted and has been through a lot of pain due to her first and second husbands. I think she has a wonderful relationship with her current husband and beautiful daughter but no grandbabies as of yet.

I have yet another sister she is the baby, and she has a lot of fond memories with me she has always been my favorite out of the last four siblings because she is the baby and she seemed to be the one I would see more than the others. I remember as I was going over to drop my son Chris off to spend the weekend, it would be her that I would see running down the hill to open the gate with her dress and pigtails flying. She seemed to have grown up fast and she has had things happen to her that made her have many hurts and wounds in her life. She has a desire to serve God and give Him every part of her, but she has many strongholds that hold her back from becoming fully committed to His call. I believe she could reach a multitude of people with her testimony and the generation of people that she has been called to if only she would bend her knee and say yes. She has issues with alcohol that outweigh her desire to serve her

God to the fullest. She needs deliverance from this in the worst way. Time is getting very short we have no time to play.

Grief

I have a few afterthoughts about grief and what it might feel like to me in certain scenarios after all that I have been through. I did not write these things about grief, and I am not sure of the author, but I got the information from Facebook. However, I wanted to use it because what it's saying could not be truer for someone who is going through tremendous grief and trauma. Grief will have you asking why all while knowing the answers could never be enough. I have so many questions, but I could never get the right answer out of anyone here on earth. Grief is feeling like death has overtaken you and you can never get that part back as long as you are here on this earth.

Grief is having to let go of what will never be again, holding on to what could have been, and trying to live in the moment of what was. I can never bring my son back and I can never see what it could have been like with him if he was still here. There are so many "I can never moments" for me that I have to put in the back of my mind. I have to think of the forever's that will take me to eternity to make it through.

Grief is the devastating feeling of guilt that comes when you think of going on without them and things that may have been said that you can never take back or things that were not said that could have been said. I have a lot of should of, could of, and would have that haunt my brain and used to come up quite frequently, but as time has marched on it doesn't come up as much. Time does heal many things, but it's always just slightly in the background looking for a moment to stand out.

Grief is the rude awakening that the rest of the world keeps moving untouched when your whole world has stopped. What was so baffling to me is that bills still have to be paid, groceries still have to be bought, and life still has to be lived. We don't know how that will be possible but something in you makes you move to do the things that must be done.

Grief looks like fear; you learn that life is fragile, and knowing this brings out anxiety and panic attacks. You feel like you are vulnerable to anything that will happen next, and you are afraid to ask what will happen next because there has been so much with yourself, your family, and your friends. This makes you feel like you will never feel normal in your own life again, so you begin to look for a new normal but then find out that normal is just a setting on your dryer, nothing more, nothing less.

Grief is waking up in the morning and losing the ones you love all over again. God says his mercies are new every morning, and I need them daily to make it. You may try to go through the daily task, and then suddenly, you are hit with a wave of sadness that takes you down. You may see a movie or hear a song that opens the floodgates to the eyes, and you pour out a river of despair, and you cannot believe what you are going through is real and that they are gone.

Grief will make you dread holidays, special days, and birthdays. You try to pretend you are ok on the outside, but inside you are torn apart and wish the day would end. These feelings will be with us to some degree for the rest of our lives and we have to learn how to work through them and know that God is with us through the pain, and he will sustain us as we give the hurt to him. The pain will subside and get better but will never totally leave. Time does make the pain even, out as you begin to learn how to walk through and live with the heaviness of that pain. Your sorrow diminishes, and you learn that tears and smiles can exist together. We must remember that the most excellent memories can never die, and for that reason, we will carry them with us eternally.

Bibliography Page

The Amplified Bible 1987, The Zondervan Corporation; Esther 4:14

The Amplified Bible 1987, The Zondervan Corporation: Isaiah 2:23

The Amplified Bible 1987, The Zondervan Corporation; Psalms 139

The Amplified Bible 1987, The Zondervan Corporation; Gen. 4:10

The Amplified Bible 1987, The Zondervan Corporation; Num. 35:33

The Amplified Bible 1987, The Zondervan Corporation; Ps. 37:5

First-Degree Murder Overview: Find law staff, Reviewed by Maddy Take, Esq June 2, 2020

Rod Stewart Reasons to Believe; Every picture tells a story album, recorded 1971 October Mercury SR-61237 Landsdowne & Olympic Studios released 1969

Johnson, Barbara (April 1, 1979) Where Does a Mother Go to Resign, Bethany Fellowship

Spafford, Horatio Gates, 1873 It is Well With My Soul.

Glorious Album

Album of Memories

My Mother

My Father

My Sister

My Brother

In Loving Memory

Chris's Father
Harrison Millwood

The End

AUTHOR PROFILE

Paula Jones

www.ingramcontent.com/pod-product-compliance
Lightning Source LLC
Chambersburg PA
CBHW060529130626
46553CB00002B/691